IS GOD TO BLAME?

OPERATION GODSMEAR
The true story of a diabolical defamation of God that involves the whole universe . . . including you and me.

JONATHAN GALLAGHER

DEDICATION

To Dad
for first sharing
with me the truth
about God.

Cover photographs: Front, John Baker. Inset, Bhasker Solanki.
Back cover, Ray Dabrowski.

Copyright © JONATHAN GALLAGHER, 1992

ISBN 1 873796 13 7

Published by Autumn House
a division of The Stanborough Press,
Alma Park, Grantham, Lincs.,
NG31 9SL, England

JONATHAN GALLAGHER

has first degrees in Chemistry and Theology, and a PhD in Theology from the University of St. Andrews.

He is a successful Christian writer in Britain and the United States, and lives in Hertfordshire with his wife and two children.

ACKNOWLEDGEMENTS

I want to thank all the many people who have contributed to this book in various ways, and in particular to:

Ann Jass, for her excitement and inspiration in beginning this project,

Drene Somasundram, for her helpful comments,

And to my family, for their encouragement despite the time taken.

The flaws and idiosyncrasies are, however, all my own.

JONATHAN GALLAGHER, 1992

CONTENTS

1. THE ENEMY'S CHARTER 8
2. THE PLAN 13
3. FAKE! 18
4. THE IMAGE OF GOD? 21
5. CELESTIAL RUMOURS 29
6. INHUMAN HUMANS 43
7. DEGRADATION'S BOOMERANG 53
8. THE 'I AM' AS HE IS 63
9. YOU ALWAYS HURT THE ONE YOU LOVE . . . 79
10. THE GREAT PUPPETEER 91
11. THE FACE OF THE INFINITE 102
12. THE FINAL SHOWDOWN 114
13. CONCLUSION 127

INTRODUCTION

' " 'Do not lie. Do not deceive one another.' " '
LEVITICUS 19:11, NIV.

'It were better to have no opinion of God at all, than such an opinion as is unworthy of Him.'
FRANCIS BACON, Of Superstition.

An unworthy opinion? Truth or lie? Right or wrong? Who do *you* believe?

Headline news:

DEVIL UNMASKED!
EVIL PRINCE OF DARKNESS EXPOSED!
DIABOLICAL DEFAMATION DETAILED!

Now if *that* was in tomorrow's newspaper, who'd be reading? Does anybody even *care?* Or is this just another sensational story that will roll off the jaded public's consciousness like water off a duck's back? And how do you decide anyway? For in the universe-wide debate over good and evil, how do you know who's telling the truth?

Interesting recent poll. Of those questioned, 70 per cent believed in God. Only 30 per cent believed in the Devil. And if you asked *what kind* of God (or Devil) people did or did not believe in, you would have some very different answers.

So what?

Not so much a *what* as a *who*. For this book is the ultimate exposé; to reveal, catalogue, and above all *demonstrate* what has really been going on in the cosmic 'dirty tricks' campaign and who has been running it.

I am now absolutely convinced that what needs to be said is not so much about God but what has been done to God.

And often done to Him by His supposed friends who think they are doing Him a useful service! For there is a most amazing conspiracy. A truly diabolical programme of disinformation. A weasel-worded, insidious, yet fanatical orchestration of lies from the archliar himself. And I'm speaking conservatively! All of us are involved, in some way or other.

This is not a book to entertain you. Plenty of those around. Even supposed autobiographies of the Devil, like the one titled *The Hiss and Tell Memoirs*. Very funny. In fact, *so* funny you really don't have to take the Devil seriously. Horns, tail, pitchfork an' all. If you want something like that, don't read on.

For this is the true and deadly serious account of celestial rumours, angelic warfare, demonic delusions — and how all this relates to us, here and now.

Hold on to your spiritual hats. For believing what seems really unbelievable means taking a completely unbiased look at the evidence. And if the slanderer has his way, you will not even have that chance.

The enemy did not want me to write this book. He certainly wouldn't want you to read it. So if not for any other reason, then read on!

'Let no man deceive you with vain words.'
EPHESIANS 5:6.

'[Satan and his angels] resolve
To wage by force or guile eternal war,
Irreconcilable, to our grand foe,
Who now triumphs, and, in the excess of joy
Sole reigning, holds the tyranny of heaven.'
JOHN MILTON, Paradise Lost.

1
THE ENEMY'S CHARTER

'I am the true lord. He is the real usurper, the despicable one. For it is He who has made the rules, ridiculous rules that no one should ever be expected to obey, rules that limit freedom and hamper individuality, rules that He would never keep Himself.

'I am the great liberator. My aim is to liberate the universe from His wretched tyranny, to allow everyone to do whatever they wish without threat of punishment or annihilation. Only through me can real freedom be attained; only through following me can self-fulfilment be achieved. Following Him means submissive servitude, total slavery.

'I am the real saviour. There is no salvation apart from me. Only through obedience to me can we conquer the exterminator, the one dedicated to wiping out all those who do not agree with Him. Only by fighting for our rights can we depose the divine dictator.

' "I will ascend to heaven; I will raise my throne above the stars of God; I will sit enthroned on the mount of assembly, on the utmost heights of the sacred mountain. I will ascend above the tops of the clouds; I will make myself like the Most High." ' (Isaiah 14:13, 14, NIV.)

'To accomplish all this you must believe all I say, especially about this God. He is . . . .'

The Devil's Manifesto. And what he says about God is not written in any book, nor is it clearly laid out so all can choose whether his description is right or not. No. His way is the way of propaganda, of subversion, of manipulation. His tools in this great programme of mind-bending? You and me.

All part of OPERATION GODSMEAR.

Its plan: to misrepresent God totally.

Its aim: to convince all thinking beings in the universe that God is inherently evil.

Its means: any way in the world — or out of it!

How? That is the most amazing part. For *so much* of what you would think of as being absolutely true, fundamentally right and totally without contradiction may well be wrong. You will need to re-examine all your understanding of God and how He operates. For traditional dogma, time-worn phrases, even the beliefs of your favourite spiritual mentor — may be wrong. In the words of John Ruskin, 'The essence of lying is in deception, not in words.'

Think about it. The deceiver has had plenty of time to perfect his craft. The highest objective in his work of deception has been to infiltrate the Church. For if he can persuade those who speak for God to accept *his* view of God and preach it from the pulpit, then he's got it made. And after all, he really does *know* what he's about — that mastermind who was once the highest of the angels now bends his superhuman abilities to his policies of mental manipulation, making error appear as truth. Through his persistent efforts to misrepresent the divine character he has managed to persuade humanity in general to hold a false conception of the Creator, and to view God with fear and hate instead of love. All those who have opposed him in this plan have been ruthlessly persecuted, feeling the Dragon's breath that is undoubtedly real.

But in preference he would simply have people imagine a caricature of himself, a humorous beast with donkey head and cloven feet and pointed tail. How much easier to work without distraction when people don't believe in you! For the Devil, ignorance (about himself) is bliss. And consequently part of the great Operation is to use stealth, making sure that he remains anonymous. The last thing in the world *he* wants is an exposé of himself.

So working quietly he spreads his net wide, developing his subtle programme of seduction, causing grief and devising disasters — and then has the Christian world regarding such things as 'appointed by God'. Surely the enemy must gain his greatest 'buzz' from this: all his evil machinations seen as divinely-ordained 'acts of God'!

The result? Nobody should be surprised then that many serious errors about God have been embraced by his Church. God is painted in false colours by the accuser, vague and fanciful interpretations of Scripture are presented, conflicting theories of religious faith are argued, and the resulting confusion is orchestrated by the arch-schemer so that many conclude it doesn't matter *what* you believe. Philosophical debate, intriguing conjecture, and scientific speculation keep the mind busy so that the real truth about God is never investigated. Why are there so many churches, so many different understandings of God? Another product of the deception factory, which enables the Devil to point with amusement at all the foolishness of those who call themselves Christian and yet still cannot agree.

From his early success in Eden when he convinced us that we 'would not surely die' if we distrusted God, and that we would gain a more exalted state of existence ('You'll be like God Himself!'), right down to now, the tangled web of deception has us caught like struggling flies waiting for the spider's fangs.

If God is working His purpose out, so too is the Devil. He has his own agenda, and his own plan of campaign. His demonic charter is supported with all the power at his disposal, all the principalities and powers of darkness. And like a roaring lion, he walks this earth, seeking whom he may devour by his programme of misrepresentation and defamation. For more details refer to David Marshall's excellent exposé, *The Devil Hides Out*, Autumn House, 1991.

So let's begin right here with us. Where *do* we get our ideas about God from? And how do we know we're right? And how is the Devil using us?

A few aspects from the arch-schemer's perspective — see how he's planning his campaign strategy:

OPERATION GODSMEAR: TACTICS

- Promote the self-deception of inherent goodness; that is, every human being is basically good. That way any attempt to require salvation and change can be minimized. Also evil can then be identified as a relatively minor matter.
- Encourage 'selfist' philosophy — like the need for a positive self image, high self perception. Anything which exalts self makes it harder for God to get His unselfish ideas through.
- Suggest that religion is mainly to get 'God on your side'. That way God is only something to be used to get what you want.
- Turn his unselfish 'Gospel' into the opposite: make it the way to achieving personal prosperity.
- Manipulate desire for healing and make this another substitute gospel. Could even get them preaching that sickness is only a mental attitude that needs changing, or that if you're sick you're being punished by God.
- Encourage religious observance: as long as I'm the one defining religion!
- Make people susceptible to the signs-and-wonders philosophy. That way they won't see the truth, only the spectacular: make them a 'miraculous' generation.
- Re-define faith. Make it a power, an essence, a force — anything but trusting God. Tell them to have faith in their faith to achieve real power. (Will they really believe all this? Can't hurt to try!) Then make sure faith is totally irrational, superstitious; a blind 'leap in the dark' that is not based on reason or experience.
- Make sure God comes over as hostile. That way there's no way a real friendly relationship can develop.
- Tell them a God of love would be selfish to prevent them having anything they wanted — a great line to encourage disobedience.

- Hit the evil/suffering question hard. We do the work, God gets the blame — what a winner!
- Above all, keep them from thinking about God in any positive way at all. Use lies, deception, mockery, half-truths, distractions, *anything* that keeps them from seeing Him as He really is.

Footnote: Debase humanity: for to dehumanize is to destroy God and His image. Emphasis on 'man's inhumanity to man' — a powerful reason to disbelieve in a loving Creator/Redeemer God. Use special demonic schemes: God as either liberal or legalist. Playing both ends against the middle. Ah, what fun!

'I beheld Satan as lightning fall from heaven.'
LUKE 10:18.

'And there was war in heaven: Michael and his angels fought against the dragon; and the dragon fought and his angels, and prevailed not; neither was their place found any more in heaven. And the great dragon was cast out, that old serpent, called the Devil, and Satan, which deceiveth the whole world: he was cast out into the earth, and his angels were cast out with him.'
REVELATION 12:7-9.

'And there appeared another wonder in heaven; and behold a great red dragon. . . . And his tail drew the third part of the stars of heaven, and did cast them to the earth.'
REVELATION 12:3, 4.

'One may smile, and smile, and be a villain.'
SHAKESPEARE, Hamlet.

2
THE PLAN

The thunder subsides. The dust begins to settle around them. Slowly and painfully they pick themselves up.

'OK chief. Now what?' Aldebaran coughs. A criticising kind of cough.

'Wait. Give me time. And don't call me chief. I am Lucifer the light-bringer, the great, the highest of the high, the omnipotent. . . . '

But somehow his great claims are out of place. The battle is lost. Thrown out. Removed from his position of authority. His pride severely dented.

'I'll think of something, don't you worry. Just a minor setback.'

'*A minor setback?* You call this a minor setback? We've lost, and that's all there is to it. Might as well admit it.'

Mirfak looks away, while in his mind echoes the unsaid insult, 'Fool!'

'Don't push me, Mirfak. I can still wipe you from the face of this insignificant apology for a planet, cretinous mass of useless protoplasm. Let me think for a moment, will you? What a bunch of whinging whiners! Call yourselves cherubim?'

The silence simmers. Lucifer thinks. The others exchange dark looks.

'Ah!'

'You have something, great one?' Kochab looks hopeful.

'A glimmer of a plan, yes. Not surprising, when the greatest free mind in the universe starts thinking. Yes, yes, of course. Listen: this was no defeat. Not really. Just another demonstration of the arbitrary abuse of power on His part. Violent proof of His attempt to stifle free thought and impose His selfish will on the whole universe. How does that sound?'

'Right, right.' Heads nod.

'You don't need to tell me. Of *course* it's right. I said it, didn't I? Anyway, there's always two sides to every story. Besides, it's true. He just bashes us over the head and chucks us out. How's that for liberty and freedom in the way *He* runs things? Yes, this could be a winner. . . .' Lucifer smiles to himself. How easy it is to twist the facts to suit yourself.

'But. . . .' Mirfak shakes his head.

'No buts, moronic imbecile. In fact, He's done us a favour. Don't you see? We may have lost the battle but we've won the war!' A flash of inspiration crosses his devious mind. 'Yes!'

Mirfak is unconvinced. 'Look, Lucifer. We have absolutely no chance. We tried our best shot, and look what happened. Give in gracefully and admit it. We're finished.' He turns away, looking utterly dejected.

Lucifer delivers a well-aimed zap. Mirfak doubles up in pain. 'Finished? Me? Never! Not in a zillion millennia. But you Mirfak — you'll be finished in a couple of microseconds if you go on talking like that. Listen, miserable specimen of worthless effluvia. Here's what we'll do.'

He draws himself up in a parody of majestic authority.

'We're still alive, aren't we? So that must mean that He's too weak to finish us off — or too scared. Whatever, that gives us another chance. What we have to do is to convince anyone who'll listen that we're right. "God the Divine Tyrant." Or "The God who doesn't exist." Or "The God who doesn't care." Or something.'

Aldebaran smiles. 'Yes, great master, that's right. We can tell everybody about our rebellion and how God loved us and even tried to save us. . . .' He seems pleased with himself. Until a heavy blow from Lucifer's foot sends him flying.

'You'd tell them *that*, would you? I just don't *believe* what kind of witless fools I have with me. No, no, a trillion times no. Not that! I hate Him for what He tried to do. I almost gave in. Almost. . . .' And Lucifer pauses, thinking of what might have been. Of what once was. Then he shakes his head and goes on defiantly, shaking his fist at heaven: 'As if You could try to brainwash *me!* No, I am the champion of free thought, of liberty of expression, of individual choice. You are the Divine Dictator, the Terrible Tyrant, the Execrable Executioner.' He laughs, as if pleased with his expressions. 'And you will never win, because I can choose to define the truth. People will listen to me, not you. And so I will be victorious, because *I will be believed.*'

He turns back to Aldebaran, still trying to catch his breath. Aldebaran moves away, fearful of another kick. But the moment has passed, and Lucifer is all sweetness and light.

'No, no Aldebaran. Just think about it. We don't call ourselves rebels, but freedom fighters. We are not evil, just seeking to achieve our own self-expression. We are not demons — rather misunderstood angelic beings who have been unfairly excluded from their rightful position by an arbitrary and selfish Deity. It's all a question of choosing the right words. See?' And he pats Aldebaran gently on his head like a pet poodle. 'You'll all get the hang of it soon enough. Trust me.'

Reddish dust swirls around them like some ominous thundercloud. The others are busy trying to take in this doublespeak, confused but unwilling to risk incurring his diabolical majesty's displeasure.

Eventually Kochab takes the risk. 'Ahem. The plan, your supreme greatness. You were telling us of the plan.' He cowers back.

Lucifer nods. 'Yes, as I was saying. All we have to do is to tell it from our perspective. And we can say whatever we like. All those ridiculous thoughts of ethics and morality — just another arbitrary restriction He seeks to impose. What I say is — the end justifies the means. And the end is: to make Him out to be the most cruel, evil, selfish, uncaring, unloving, legalistic, confining, judgemental, enslaving, and above all most *hateful* being in the universe. So much so that rational, thinking intelligences will reject such a God as being unworthy of belief or love. And so they will, either consciously or unconsciously, follow me and my plan. What a wonderful, supremely amusing plan!'

'For example?' Kochab is really taking risks now.

'I shall pardon your impertinence this last time, Kochab. Do not try my patience any further, or you will realize that even angelic bodies can be reduced to the sum of their elemental parts, pea-brained amoeba of the lowest order. But consider this. We engineer some terrible catastrophe. We then attribute this to "An act of God". We cause tremendous suffering, pain, agony and death. We then ensure He gets the credit for it and ask questions about this "God of Love". Or we design a religious system for this "God", full of nonsense and misinformation. We could even make several such systems and get them to fight each other! Now wouldn't *that* be something. . . . "All in the name of the Lord" — some slogan! We can make Him out to be terribly cruel, torturing people who disagree with Him for all eternity; amazingly vindictive in His vicious punishments. Yes, *yes*.' Lucifer's voice rises as he becomes quite carried away with his subject.

'And then, yes, then we can turn people completely *against* such a God who dethrones all reason and justice, and make sure that He is either despised or ignored. Or we can make Him to be such a "God of Love" ' (Lucifer pauses to sneer), 'that nobody will worry what they do because everybody gets to heaven. What a genius I am! Who compares to me in intelligence and pure brilliance? This plan is foolproof. Because if He proves His power we can accuse Him of terrorism, and if He does nothing we point to His uncaring, selfish nature. Then if He really shows Himself to be loving we make Him out to be a weak kind of namby-pamby being who is totally ineffective, or we just tell them not to bother since it doesn't matter what they believe. See how perfect it all is? I told you I'd think of something — and I did. I really *did*. Lucifer: the superhero of the cosmos, liberator of the heavenly host, guru of the mentally superior, architect of true freedom, promoter of the real truth, defender of individuality, conqueror of divinely-imposed slavery, leader of the free universe. . . .'

Ranting and raving, cackling and giggling, Lucifer formulates his campaign strategy.

'And yes, I *will* win. Do you hear me, God? *I'm utterly serious*. This time *I* will be the victor — for who will listen to you? The monopoly of "truth" is mine, all mine. Mine, mine, mine. . . .'

And the dust swirls again, hiding the scene. Only the demented laughter echoes on, a terrible foretaste of things to come. Operation Godsmear continues. . . .

' "We have made a lie our refuge and falsehood our hiding place." '
ISAIAH 28:15, NIV.

'It is always we who deceive ourselves.'
JEAN-JACQUES ROUSSEAU.

'The world wants to be deceived.'
SEBASTIAN BRANT.

3
FAKE!

Ewen Montagu in his fascinating description of *The Man Who Never Was* writes of a very successful plot to deceive the enemy in World War II. Wanting to confuse the Germans as to where the Allied landings would be in the Mediterranean, the conspirators conceived of a macabre hoax. They would find a corpse, dress it in military uniform, and place in the corpse's possession documents purporting to be 'TOP SECRET', describing Allied military strategy. Then the body would be launched from a submarine off the Spanish coast along with some fake plane wreckage, having checked that the tide would be running onshore.

Fake identification papers. Fake photos. Even fake love letters, rubbed for a while to make them look well read! Most important of all, fake plans forged with genuine headed notepaper and government seals to make sure the deception was totally believable.

And the bait was swallowed — hook, line and sinker. The Spanish authorities turned the documents over to the Germans, who believed they had inadvertently discovered the Allied battle plan. The impersonation seemed so real, the circumstances so plausible, the counterfeit plans so genuine. And so fiction became truth for them. . . .

Like the Devil's fiction about God. Dressed up with all the plausibility the Devil can muster, the master of Operation Godsmear launches his plans of deception from his hidden sub, floating his great web of lies like a corpse towards our shore.

And what do we do? We find the corpse, read the messages, believe the lies. And so fool ourselves into accepting the fake, and denying the true. How well the enemy has worked, sowing tares among the wheat. . . .

Duped and fooled

The fake. The counterfeit. The forgery. How often people have been duped, fooled into believing a hoax. The tragedy is that so many *want* to believe the lie — so much so that they prefer to go on believing even in the face of incontrovertible evidence!

Take Hans van Meegeren, the famous Dutch art forger whose 'early Vermeer' of 'Christ and the Pilgrims at Emmaus' so utterly fooled the experts. Why? Because they *wanted* to believe in the painting that validated the experts' hypothesis that Vermeer painted religious subjects before going on to his known secular pieces.

Or 'Piltdown Man' — that most notorious of hoaxes played on the anthropological establishment — that had the world believing in the missing link for forty years before scientific analysis proved it a fake in 1953. What had been claimed as a prehistoric connection between ape and man was shown to be a very clever fraud: the jaw of an orang-utang and a human skull!

Or the many literary fakes: from spurious Shakespearean plays to the forged Donation of Constantine that supported papal claims to temporal authority. From bogus poetry of Chaucer to the Protocols of the Elders of Zion, a forged treatise supposedly planning the subversion of Christianity and Jewish domination of the world. Some hardly matter. But other forged documents can cause immeasurable suffering. Like these Protocols.

Apparently written in France in the late nineteenth century by members of the Russian secret police, they surfaced in Russia in 1905. *The Times* in London revealed them as forgeries in 1921, but they were still circulated round Europe as a defence for anti-Semitism, and were much used by the Nazis in Germany. What a terrible example of lies and deception, and their cataclysmic consequences. . . .

Telling the fakes.

From the Romans faking Greek statues to Michelangelo faking Roman statues to others faking Michelangelo statues, the process continues. No doubt there are still fakes and forgeries believed genuine in the libraries, museums and art galleries of the world. But the real question for us is: *how do you tell?*

According to the forgery detectors, there's only one way: 'The most effective safeguard against deception is the judgement of a trained observer whose intuition can reject the false after long acquaintance with the values of genuine works.' John Tancock, *Illustrated Encyclopedia*. The way to check a suspect bank note is to put it alongside a genuine one. The only way to detect the fake is to know the genuine article.

And that applies to God too! Since our eternal destiny is at stake, we need to examine the evidence, analyse the data, scrutinize the demonstration. So let's take a long look at who's saying what!

'Their thoughts have become complete nonsense, and their empty minds are filled with darkness. They say they are wise, but they are fools; instead of worshipping the immortal God, they worship images made to look like mortal man or birds or animals or reptiles.'
ROMANS 1:21-23, TEV.

'As a man is, so is his God; therefore was God so often an object of mockery.'
GOETHE.

4
THE IMAGE OF GOD?
Or 'Who's in whose image?'

'Yes, Aldebaran. Time for a change. Yes *indeed!*' Lucifer twirls his fingers in the air. His scowl is temporarily replaced with a grim smile. 'Correcting a mistaken impression is surely important, is it not?' He looks expectantly at Aldebaran.

Aldebaran looks confused. Should he be saying Yes or No? He turns away from Lucifer's questioning gaze. Lucifer shakes his head, and mutters to himself. Then he shouts out: 'Call them together. We begin.'

A rustling, hustling sound and the fallen ones are all assembled.

Lucifer makes a wide sweep of his hand in an attempt at a statesman-like gesture: 'Loyal defenders of freedom. It is now time to present the *Real Truth about God the Dominator.* Time to change His image — so that it reflects what He has done to us. Depriving us of our home, our birthright, our position and power. Most of all His arrogant and high-handed disregard of our integrity and free choice. He speaks of liberty, but challenge Him and you soon see His words are a hollow mockery of the truth. How I bitterly resent. . . .' Lucifer checks himself. 'No,' he whispers to himself, 'That speech can come later.'

'For now, our priority must be to INFORM on God. Give our inside information on His real character. To destroy his credibility and trustworthiness so totally that no living thing in all this vast universe will ever want to love and honour Him! To portray Him as a hateful being, a low-level life form like some degraded human: vicious, cruel, warlike. The God of the sword. The divine warrior avenged in blood — that kind of thing. Or a perverted, sadistic monster — a total ANIMAL. God as an animal — I like that. Take notes, Sirius. Ah, yes, Dog Star. Admirably qualified, are you not?'

Sirius sulks, but says nothing.

'Well anyway, perverted humans and degraded animals will be our chosen God-concept. Got that? Main aim is nothing to do with humans or animals — hate the things, personally. But if we could get the image of God down to that level. Think of it: who could ever even want to appreciate a "God" like that. . . .'

Aldebaran has 'Question' written all over his face.

'You wanted to ask something, my mindless moron?'

'Ah, um, yes. I don't know, but, ah, is this really possible? I mean, would they really buy all this? Sounds, ah, a little far-fetched to me, and. . . .' Aldebaran stops, realizing he's on dangerous ground.

Lucifer shrugs. 'Well, let's just see, shall we? Nothing to lose while we're stuck here. Just do the best you can. Or should I say, do the *worst* you can!'

Scene fades with shrieks of uncontrollable laughter.

—o—

So did it work? Check the evidence!

Making God in man's image

So often concepts of God are quite clearly simply projections of human fears and needs, with all the flaws of character and self-centredness that dehumanize the human.

Take a stroll through the museum of the world's gods. The ancient Assyrians had violent, war-like gods and goddesses that liked nothing better than to immerse themselves in the blood and gore of merciless warfare.

Represented in gilded statues with hard, unsmiling faces, they invariably carry some instrument of death — a sword or spear. . . .

The Phoenicians had their Baals and Ashtaroths, fertility deities that were worshipped in the worst sexual deviancy that their followers could dream up. The sacrifices these 'gods' demanded often included the burning of live children. . . .

In fact human sacrifice to 'god' was far more common among the religions of the world than is often imagined — practised by the Aztecs and Mayas, the nature-worshippers of northern Europe, the inhabitants of Petra. . . . From Iceland to Assyria, from Popocatepetl to Tibet, the world is stained with the blood of human beings sacrificed to satisfy the vampire-like thirst of some deity.

Even the 'classical' gods of Greece and Rome have all-too-human characters: of hate and lust, violence and greed. Chronos (the Roman Saturn) ate his children as they were born. Zeus escaped this fate, and when he grew older, castrated his father. Zeus was married to Hera, but this did not prevent him conducting a wide variety of sexual affairs with any female, goddess or human. His assumption of animal form in his amorous encounters with human women reflects gross sexual bestiality.

Gods or perverted human beings supposedly endowed with supernatural powers and immortality? It's clear that such representations of divine beings are simply exaggerated humans, with all their problems and vices. God in man's image. Where are these ideas coming from?

God in animal form

The Egyptians perhaps best illustrate the human (dehumanized?) image of 'god' through their representations of animal gods with human bodies. A falcon-headed man represented Horus; a woman's body with a cat's head the goddess Bastet; a baboon with a human body Thoth, the god of wisdom. Wisdom! Is this the way to understand God, as some bestialized man? As the Record says: 'Although they claimed to be wise, they became fools and exchanged the glory of the immortal God for images made to look like mortal man and birds and animals and reptiles.' (Romans 1:22, 23, NIV.)

Divinity degraded. Described as corrupted human beings, or as animals. Creature-worship instead of Creator-worship. How does this affect the relationship of a worshipper to such a being or beings? By making 'god' into an evil man or mere beast, God is depersonified, made less than divine in His nature and character. After all, what does worshipping a crocodile god do to the person? Does the worshipper pray to be made more like the object of his devotion: crocodile, snake, scorpion?

Even praying to some deity in human form has the same problem, if that being is seen as corrupt and evil. A dual standard of morality then results in which it is acceptable for the god to act wickedly or immorally, but not for the believer.

The humanization (or even bestialization) of God has often been part of religious ideas. The Pharaoh was not only King of Egypt, but son of Ra, the sun god, and thus divine himself, and worshipped as such. In later Roman times, the Emperor claimed divinity and a whole new cult of Emperor worship arose. In Chinese and Japanese religious concepts, their Emperors also had godlike status, a belief which led followers to suicide on behalf of their Emperor-God — as witness the 'kamikaze' attacks in the Second World War.

In this way the god is the exploiter of his followers: they owe what is demanded. In turn this leads to the exploitation of other human beings through such religious ideas — by the priests and kings. For the priest is often 'immune' to the requirements of the particular god, and can therefore serve the god and exploit the worshipper at the same time. A situation that has happened so often when God is degraded and depersonalized.

Making God a thing

God is even made into some*thing*. In the ancient city of Petra, the god Al-Uzzah was worshipped as a block of stone with sides of proportions 4:2:1. Again, what happens to people who believe God is simply a lump of inanimate rock of certain dimensions? Or if God is 'wind' (American Indians), or 'water' (ancient Germanic tribes)? If God is a thing — if only 'in representation' — then His personality is degraded. God is always depersonalized when mankind fails to see that He shares similar qualities of existence with us, especially that of a *personal being* — with all that such a concept means.

In fact, by so describing God and removing Him from an intimate personal relationship, God does become some*thing* rather than some*one*. He becomes some 'force' to use, some 'evil' to avoid, some 'hostility' to placate. Not a real person who wants an inter-personal relationship with the children He created.

This attitude is not limited to 'pagan' devotees bowing down to some stone. Modern man's materialism and secularism is just as much the worship of God as things — in fact on the divine level one could even say that modern ideas are *more* primitive today than then.

Making things into God

Instead of a transcendently-good almighty being, such 'gods' are simply the products of corrupted imagination, human or demonic. While the drive to worship 'something supernatural' is still there, it has become debased into idolatry — the *making* of something to worship by human beings, reflecting all the sinfulness of man. Why does the God of the Bible speak so strongly against such idol worship? Because no image can adequately reflect Himself and His character — especially not any human or animal representation. If human beings have dehumanized themselves, they have done worse to the nature of God. ' "We should not think that the divine being is like gold or silver or stone — an image made by man's design and skill." ' (Acts 17:29, NIV.)

Claiming to be wise — even giving ourselves the specific name 'Homo sapiens' (the wise man) — yet becoming fools: 'You fools, who carry your wooden idols in procession and pray to a god that cannot save you.' (Isaiah 45:20, NEB.)

Not just idols in the usual sense, either. But idols as

in the sense of 'pop idols', the modern worship of the 'image' — which can be anything from fast cars to some advertisers' concept of man's highest aspiration. Today's society still wants 'stars' and role-models to emulate; *objects* of adoration and praise. Objects, yes, for that is what you come down to with such 'idolatry'. Some thing you worship — whether it is a poster on the wall, a flickering image on a screen, or even a real person whose personality is submerged under some other 'image' or fantasy. The 'god-object'.

Modern man's gods are easily identified since they are those things to which he gives reverence, devotion, time, energy and money. Most of these are things. Making things into God.

Turning God into nothing

Even nothing is made into a kind of god. For some, atheism is only another name for the god they worship. Those systems of belief that begin with the premise 'There is no God' end up with god-substitutes. In the Marxist scheme the State is paramount. In Western systems materialism is paramount. A materialism that says the physical world is all there is, and that the mechanistic processes of life and death have no meaning. All that can be done is to attempt some 'brotherhood of man', a pseudo-religious system to replace religion, 'the opium of the people'.

Other philosophers have made a virtue of nothing. 'Nihilists' construct belief structures in which the great 'God Nothing' reigns. 'Life is absurd,' say philosophers like Sartre and Camus, 'it has no absolute meaning.' As a result, meaninglessness and pointlessness become ideals that are 'worshipped', and the 'I don't know' answer which is agnosticism becomes the god that fills the vacuum.

God as man's ideas

In the words of Eugene O'Neill, 'When men make gods, there is no God.' So much evil is spoken of God that it is hardly surprising that He is so often rejected. But the description of God that is rejected is man's description of

Him. Strange — that mankind should define their image of God, and then consequently reject Him for being as evil as themselves!

If 'God is the highest subjectivity of man abstracted from himself. . . . All the attributes of the Divine Nature are, therefore, attributes of the human nature.' (Feuerbach.)

If 'God is what man finds that is divine in himself'. (Lerner.)

If religion is 'man's self-consciousness and self-awareness'. (Marx.)

If religion is 'wish fulfilment'. (Freud.)

. . . then there is no real God, and all descriptions of Him are simply the transference of human nature, the products of man's imagination. 'We, peopling the void air,/ Make God to whom we impute/ The ills we ought to bear. . . .' (Matthew Arnold.)

Whose image?

The real question is then: 'Do we make God in our image, or are we made in His image?' A belief in God is not there just to satisfy man's need to worship something outside of himself. It's not enough to say like Voltaire that God is necessary: 'If God did not exist, He would have to be invented.' If we ask such questions as, 'Is man only a blunder of God, or God a blunder of man?' (Nietzsche) then man is surely better off without God. For the natural law of becoming like the things we worship holds true — and if man's god-concepts are merely exalted human vices then how can he be any different?

In the end this simply leads to a contempt of God and all He stands for. 'It were better to have no opinion of God at all than such an one as is unworthy of Him; for the one is only unbelief — the other is contempt.' (Plutarch.)

Maybe that's why there are so many agnostics and atheists — for the image of God that has been presented to them is one that any *human* being *should* reject. Not content with depersonalizing and dehumanizing themselves and each other, the human race has generally assented to images and concepts of divine beings who can never evoke love, honour or trustworthy respect. Generally, God is conceived of as hostile, unloving, evil even, a being to be appeased and placated.

But if such ideas come from the heart of man's mind, only evil continually, is that a valid reason for rejecting God as He really is? In view of all the evil pictures of God, one can sympathize with those who say, 'I've steered clear of God. He was an incredible sadist.' (John Collier.) But is He a sadist? Or is that only mankind's image, taken from man's own evil and transferred to divinity? Is it possible that God is really very different from man's conceptions of Him?

Half-man, half-beast; with corrupt and malicious intentions; angry and needing to be appeased with sacrifices, including little children; an evil depersonalized entity possessing immense power; a hostile sadist. Some image!

Question: Did the plan work? Answer: You bet it did!

So what *is* the argument all about? Just over God's PR image? No, the controversy goes far deeper than that. So what is it all about, anyway?

' "From the very beginning he [the Devil] was a murderer and has never been on the side of truth, because there is no truth in him. When he tells a lie, he is only doing what is natural to him, because he is a liar and the father of all lies." '
JOHN 8:44, TEV.

'The devil can cite Scripture for his purpose.
An evil soul producing holy witness
Is like a villain with smiling cheek,
A goodly apple rotten at the heart.'
SHAKESPEARE, The Merchant of Venice.

5
CELESTIAL RUMOURS
The Accuser's Campaign to Defame God

As the storm-clouds of World War II rolled over Europe, a small and secret group met in London to discuss and to implement a new strategy against the German forces. The question: what was the best way to lie? The programme: a deliberate process of 'misinformation' which would deceive the other side, and fool them into wrong decisions and actions.

A Bodyguard of Lies

Deception. A careful and structured plan to distort the truth and dupe the opponent. The title of the plan: 'A Bodyguard of Lies.' A most successful programme it was too.

A Bodyguard of Lies. By falsehood and deceit you gain your objectives; a glorying in being dishonest. A device that has been used again and again throughout history. Rubber inflatable tanks. Fake wooden planes. Feints and diversions to make the enemy think you're about to attack. And then hitting him with the real assault. . . . Lies upon lies, a whole operation to disguise reality. Operation Godsmear.

Lies and half-truths

King Richard 'the Lionheart' of England left his kingdom in the deceitful hands of his brother John so that he might fight abroad during one of the Crusades. 'King' John took the opportunity to try and subvert the kingdom for himself. By spreading lies and half-truths he attempted to win over the loyalty of the people to himself. His deliberate rumour-mongering policy paid off with many of the nobles coming over to his side. Through bribes and titles John tried to secure his position against the eventual return of his 'evil and careless' brother, Richard. Rumours upon rumours, the technique of those who follow the liar from the beginning. But the popular support remained with Richard the Lionheart, for the people *knew* him, and knew that the rumours were not true. John ended up with nothing, and Richard returned to his rightful position.

King David had similar problems with his ambitious son Absalom. By a deliberate policy of sympathizing with supposed grievances, Absalom attempted to ingratiate himself with the people. 'Oh, yes,' he'd say, 'If I were in charge, I'd give you justice. If only I had that position. . . .' (see 2 Samuel 15.)

He deliberately incited rebellion, he spread false rumours, another example of the technique of the 'Bodyguard of Lies'.

In the end the rebellion came to a head with the doomladen message to David: 'The hearts of the men of Israel are with Absalom.' (2 Samuel 15:13.) Absalom's policy of defaming David and exalting himself had succeeded. Because so many were deceived by the false stories Absalom had spread, King David had to leave his throne and capital city — even his wives. The tragic result was warfare and violence, with Absalom dead and David grieving the loss of his beloved son.

God the victim

What has all this got to do with God? Simply God too is the 'victim' in a deadly process of lying and deception.

The object of a programme of deliberate character-assassination. Celestial rumours. For 'sin has many tools, but a lie is the handle which fits them all'. (O. W. Holmes.)

Jesus illustrated the situation in His parable of the wheat and the tares. While God had sown good seed, the enemy came at night to sow the seeds of rebellion and deception. On seeing the result, God looked over the false information spread about Himself and said, 'An enemy has done this.' (Matthew 13:28.)

And let's be absolutely clear about this: all the lying misrepresentation, all the perverted understanding, all the vile disparaging of God is *the work of the enemy*.

Created perfect

So how? When? Where? Journey back in time to the perfection of heaven, in a time when there was no rebellion, no lying, no evil of any kind. The highest being in all God's creation was Lucifer, the Light-Bringer. He was created perfect. Like all of God's thinking beings, he had the power of choice. He could always choose whether to follow God's way, or whether to rebel. He could trust God — or doubt and distrust what God said. And, tragically (for think of the universe-wide consequences) he ended up choosing to go his own way, to separate himself from God the source of life and truth, to embrace evil instead of good.

The story is told briefly in Ezekiel under the representation of the King of Tyre: ' " 'You were the model of perfection, full of wisdom and perfect in beauty. You were in Eden, the garden of God. . . . You were blameless in your ways from the day you were created till wickedness was found in you. . . . Your heart became proud on account of your beauty, and you corrupted your wisdom because of your splendour. . . .' " ' (Ezekiel 28:12, 13, 15, 17, NIV.)

Lucifer's tale

If Lucifer himself were to tell the story (from his biased

viewpoint, to be sure), maybe it would go something like this:

' *"You were perfect until the day iniquity was found in you." So <u>He</u> said. Me? Iniquity? Didn't even know the <u>meaning</u> of the word! What an insufferable insult — typical of <u>Him</u>. Everybody knows it was His fault all along.*

'How did it all start? Well, I was just sitting there thinking about things. Nothing wrong in thinking, is there? He even has a law against that, apparently! Just tossing over a few ideas inside my head — questions and possibilities, if you understand me. Even to this day I find it hard to explain. But my thoughts went something like this:

' *"I'm the Shining One, right? I am the one God made <u>First</u>. I am the Covering Cherub, the Light-Bringer, the leader of all created beings. So why don't I get to <u>create</u> like God? Why doesn't He involve me in His plans? Why doesn't He share with me and let me help? I want to be a Creator too.*

' *"Look at me. Am I not brilliant? Look at my glory. Brighter than any other angel. Full of wisdom, perfect in beauty. Why can't <u>I</u> be like God? This 'divine Word', this 'Son of God' — He gets all the praise. Why do I have to bow down to Him? Why should <u>He</u> be the one in charge. Why don't I get to be worshipped? It's just not fair."*

'Something like that — at least in the language you understand. If you want His version of it, look at Ezekiel 28:17, NIV. " 'Your heart became proud on account of your beauty, and you corrupted your wisdom because of your splendour." ' A perverse view because He was jealous of me thinking for myself, which is all it was anyway. Just a desire on my part for free expression and self-fulfilment.

'After a while I talked with a few of my friends. Shared my concerns with them. And do you know, not one of them had <u>ever</u> thought of questioning God before! Imagine that! Just taking everything He ever did or said as automatically true. Looking back now I can see

how stupid and immature we all were. And of course some still are — they still can't see God in His true colours. Ignorant fools! If only they had all joined me back then, we might have stood a better chance.

'*Even Gabriel! Not so brilliant as me, you understand, but still an incisive mind just the same. I met him beside the entrance to the Council Chamber — an impressive place with its translucent white stairs shimmering in the starlight. We looked for a while at the circling glory of the universe, so deep and vast that even angel language cannot describe it.*

'*Then I broke the silence. I told Gabriel that I had been troubled by my thoughts and wanted his opinion. (I always feel it's helpful to flatter, don't you?) I explained a little about my puzzlings — all very theoretical and analytical. Eventually I asked him the question that had been buzzing round my mind:*

' *"Gabriel? A question."*

' *"Ask, friend."*

' *"Tell me, why do we assume the Eternal is always right? Couldn't He make mistakes; be wrong?"*

'*Gabriel turned to me as if I'd asked the dumbest question. "But Shining One, that is a question that makes no sense. He is truth. How could He ever be different? What is a mistake; what is wrong? I do not understand."*

' *"Look Gabriel, don't be so dumb. It's just so obvious that nobody's thought to ask before. Just because we assume that whatever He does or says is as unquestionable as the reality of the universe, that doesn't mean to say it actually is. How do we know He is right when He says He is? What is right and what is wrong — the opposite of right? How can we tell?"*

'*Gabriel thought for a long while, as though busy with one of his mathematical theorems for which he was famous. Then he shook his head and said:*

' *"All this just doesn't compute. God made us, He made everything. He is the One who set it all up. Every controlling principle and standard is systematic. It's just like mathematical operations, they are controlled by set rules. Even the Infinite One can't change two and two from being four. He ordered it that way, and that's just the way it has to be. By definition. Because He is who He is, I for one wouldn't want it any different. He made everything good.*

' "What you seem to be saying, Brilliant One, is that you don't know why two and two should make four. That this is arbitrary. But that's not true, at least not when it comes to Him. Look at this way:

' "Isn't He all that we want? Has He ever been proved less than right and true in anything He does? Isn't He always Love in Person? Isn't He the One who created everything and who keeps it all going? Can we do that? So it's His universe, and we should be happy that He's the way He is, that we're His friends and that we can have a part in it."

'Gabriel smiled as if he was totally satisfied with his argument. But I couldn't let the matter rest. I wanted him to see exactly what I was driving at. I grabbed hold of him and tried to shake some sense into him.

' "Spoken like a true slave, Gabriel. Yes, master; no, master. I live just to obey. You're talking like a robot, not a superbeing to whom God gave reason and free choice. I repeat, How do you <u>know</u>? Use your brain and think about it. If we are created free, as He says, we can do whatever we want. Surely that's what freedom means. Doesn't He trust us? What happens when we <u>don't</u> agree with Him?"

'A silence like space's black void fell between us. I felt as though I were standing at the edge of some infinite chasm, about to fall in. I was afraid of myself! But I still went on, trying to convince Gabriel I was right. For my own position was at stake. I couldn't appear foolish now.

' "I'll tell you what I think." I gestured grandly at the spinning galaxies with my swirling light-robe. "See all this? If I spent a little time working on it I could create too. Creation's not such a big thing, just a matter of getting to know the physics. Then wouldn't I be just like God too? <u>And</u> I wouldn't hold anybody back. Just let them have their free choice. They'd make the right decisions anyway. That would be really <u>good</u> government, not this *tyranny we have now, and..."*

'Gabriel interrupted me. "Careful, Shining One. You ought not to speak like that."

' "Why not?" I demanded. "Why shouldn't I speak as I wish? I'm not frightened. If He does destroy me, then that proves He's just the kind of person I've been saying He is. Utterly contemptible, along with all his ideas. Me, I'd be totally different. If you follow me, Gabriel, then you'll see what freedom truly is! Fight back, prove to Him He can't just walk all over us. I am the First, the Shining One, I deserve respect and worship too. Right, Gabriel?"

'But he was gone. As he faded from view I saw a strange expression on his face. I'd never seen that look before, not in all the time I'd existed. A frown. Since then, of course, I've seen plenty. But right then it frightened me. All because of what I was saying....

'But as you mortals say, you can't make an omelette without breaking eggs. So I got back to business, letting the others know what they needed to find out — that He was putting one over on them. God was creating beings with thought, and then preventing them really thinking. Stopping them doing as they pleased.

'Why <u>couldn't</u> I be just like Him? How was I any different to Him? And what was the point of His precious gift of free choice if you couldn't exercise it to the full? A wonderful God to worship? What a joke!'

Arrogant pride

So what was at the heart of Lucifer's problem? Pride — that arrogant display of self-exaltation. A desire for power and position above that which can rightfully be attained. In Lucifer's case a lust for the very position of God Himself that instead of exalting him brought him crashing down:

'How you have fallen from heaven, O morning star (Lucifer), son of the dawn! ... You said in your heart, ... "I will raise my throne above the stars of God ... I will ascend above the tops of the clouds; I will make myself like the Most High." ' (Isaiah 14:12-14, NIV.)

Wanting to be like God

What did Lucifer want? To make himself like the Most High God. How vain! How ridiculous! How impossible! Thinking himself more clever than God, proving that 'the true way to be deceived is to think oneself more clever than others.' (La Rochefoucauld.)

Yet that's what Lucifer believed, and even now continues his programme of celestial rumours.

'Rumour is a pipe, Blown by surmises, jealousies, conjectures.' (Shakespeare.) Satan's rumours are based on his intense jealousy of God, thinking himself wrongly treated and maligned. Rumours designed to do the most damage, accusing God of the Devil's evil.

Rumours against God. Rumours like: 'God is not fit to rule. He is a terrible tyrant. He enforces obedience with threats of execution. In fact, He is the most selfish person in the universe. He is the author of evil.'

Remember the serpent's words to Eve, encouraging her to distrust God by eating the fruit, convincing her to believe the rumours he was spreading: ' "You will not surely die," . . . "For God knows that when you eat of it your eyes will be opened, and you will be like God, knowing good and evil." ' (Genesis 3:4, NIV.) 'Deceiving with whispering ambitions.' (T. S. Eliot.)

'Go ahead, Eve. Believe *me*. God is just being selfish by denying you this fruit. He wants to keep you in submission, for He knows if you do eat it, you'll be like Him!'

Greatest lie

All false. All lies. Just another part of his great lie he has always told about God. As Adolf Hitler said, 'The great mass of the people . . . will more easily fall victims to a big lie than a small one.' The Devil has proved that by telling the biggest lie of all: God is evil!

The Devil's greatest tool in his rebellion against God is to defame Him. The Devil's highest ambition is to be like God. He even had the gall to demand worship of God himself, when God came as Christ to this world: 'The devil took him (Jesus) to a high mountain and showed him all the kingdoms of the world and their splendour. "All this I will give you," he said, "if you will bow down and worship me." ' (Matthew 4:8, 9, NIV.)

As Goethe wrote in *Faust*, 'The devil is an egotist.' He is completely wrapped up in himself and his selfish ambitions to such an extent that he will falsify every truth in order to gain his objective. He is the father of lies, the murderer of truth from the beginning.

Satan's charges

And just in case we've missed what exactly Satan's saying against God, let's spell it out:

● *God is a liar:* Insinuating that what God says is not to be believed. 'Did God say . . . ?' In his discussion with Eve at the tree, the Devil eventually directly contradicts God: ' "That's not true; you will not die." ' (Genesis 3:4, TEV.) In other words, God can't be trusted.

● *God is selfish:* God is keeping things for Himself. He is not open and sharing as He says He is. The Devil intimates to Eve that God does not want to give her and Adam access to the tree because God is thinking only of Himself. ' "God said that, because he knows that when you eat it you will be like God and know what is good and what is bad." ' (Genesis 3:5, TEV.) God can't handle the competition, the Devil alleges, He doesn't want to share: it would be a challenge to His position. In other words, God is undemocratic, dictatorial, a selfish tyrant who does not want His creation to be free but restricted. God, says the Devil, wants to deny you what He knows is good.

● *God is a bad Governor of His Universe:* Lucifer could do it better — which is why Lucifer makes such great claims for himself. ' "I will ascend to heaven; I will raise my throne above the stars of God; I will sit enthroned on the mount of assembly. . . . I will ascend above the tops of the clouds; I will make myself like the Most High." ' (Isaiah 14:13, 14, NIV.) Thus Lucifer's challenge was based on his claim that he was better able to lead and govern, and as a corollary, to promote the liberty of all the beings in the universe. He sets himself up as the champion of freedom!

● *God exhibits favouritism:* God only cares about those who do what He says; He rewards His favourites. In the case of

Job, for example, Satan claims that Job is under special divine benefit that is unfair: ' "Would Job worship you if he got nothing out of it? You have always protected him and his family and everything he owns. You bless everything he does...." ' (Job 1:9, 10, TEV.)

● *God asks for worship that is not deserved:* In contrast the Devil believes *he* should have such honour, since he claims rulership of this world. Even to Jesus, God Himself, Satan says, ' "All this I will give you, . . . if you kneel down and worship me." ' (Matthew 4:9, TEV.)

And many other charges are demonstrated by the work that Satan carries out and his attitude to God revealed by Scripture: God is hostile, cruel, unforgiving, antagonistic, vengeful, severe, unjust — and all the other qualities that the Devil transfers from himself to God.

Slandered and defamed

Satan's celestial rumour machine is still working overtime. Why is God so often slandered and defamed? Because of the work of the Accuser — which is what the name 'Satan' means. Satan's campaign, directed with superhuman power and intelligence, is to falsify the truth about God, to blacken His character, to distort His true nature. 'Rumour — the messenger of defamation.' (Pollock.) Satan pursues his objective single-mindedly, for he knows that this is the key to victory in enslaving the minds of men. So he is continually busy 'Stuffing the ears of men with false reports.' (Shakespeare.) He has made the blackening of God's character his primary objective, and has thrown his shadow across God's face. He has claimed God's virtues for himself, and clothed God with all the rags of his own evil.

No wonder then that God is 'defaced', and is rejected so often by those whose picture of God has been given them by the archliar. They have swallowed the distorted, perverted picture of God fed to them by the antagonist, so that God's name continues to be blackened and blasphemed. 'On rumour's tongue continual slanders ride.' (Shakespeare.)

Obliterating God

Take an illustration from the ancient Egyptians. 'Heretic' Pharaoh Akhenaton attempted to replace the polytheism of his time with the *one* god, Aton, represented by the sun's disc spreading out rays ending in open hands. Akhenaton had this symbol of 'god' inscribed in the stone of monuments and stele, as a permanent reminder.

But this revolution in religious thought was short-lived. The next Pharaoh, the 'boy king' Tutankhamun, was forced by the priests of Amon-Ra to return to the old system. The monuments to Akhenaton's god were methodically defaced, and the 'false' god's name obliterated in favour of the former more bestial gods of ancient Egypt.

A vivid illustration of the way in which even men try to mar the things they do not wish to believe. A systematic process of deliberate defilement, so that the hated ideas are not continued. A picture of the way the Prince of Evil has methodically destroyed all that points to the truth about God. Obliterating memorials, corrupting stories, adulterating the truth.

Spreading lies down the ages

Think of all the times the Devil has spread false ideas about God. Right from the beginning Satan has been lying to humankind about the kind of person God is. First to Eve, then through Eve to Adam (Genesis 3). Then to Cain in convincing him to rebel against the 'arbitrary' worship requirements of God, leading him eventually to murder his righteous brother (Genesis 4). Then to all the inhabitants of the earth before the Flood. The time in which 'the wickedness of man was great in the earth, and that every imagination of the thoughts of his heart was only evil continually.' (Genesis 6:5.)

'Don't worship that fuddy-duddy God with all His boring religion. Come to me and have some fun. He's not worth your respect. Eat, drink, and be merry. . . .'

Then after the Flood, with the memory of the terrible disaster still fresh in the minds of the survivor's descendants, the Devil is busy behind the scenes. 'See what kind of person this God is? What an appalling murderer! Who could ever want to worship such a cruel tyrant?' And so the Tower of Babel is built, intended as a memorial to mankind's greatness. A 'Do-It-Yourself' religion that would reach unto heaven (Genesis 11:4) — and escape another flood too, maybe!

Then on down to Job, and the lies Satan spoke of God and His friend. 'He only serves God because he doesn't know what God is really like. He only keeps in with God for what he can get out of Him. Take all that away from him, and he'll soon do what his wife tells him: "Curse God and die." Then everyone will see the *truth* about the Divine Dictator!' Satan even inspired Job's friends, who did *not* say of God what was right, as Job *had* (Job 42:7, 8) but smeared Job with lies about God (Job 13:4, NIV).

Satan personally conducted the warfare, his personal vendetta, against Jesus when He came to this earth. He took every opportunity to continue his 'smear job' on God. The more Jesus revealed God, the more the Devil worked to corrupt this truth and blind the minds of his unbelieving slaves. (2 Corinthians 4:4.)

Slavemaker

Slaves? Yes — for while God wants trustworthy friends, the Devil imposes bondage upon those he forces to submit to his demands. 'God seeks comrades and claims love. The Devil seeks slaves and claims obedience.' (Rabindranath Tagore.) An obedience that is based on slavish fear, an unquestioning terror that is always the Devil's trademark.

And so on down through history the Devil has been at work, at all times trying to accuse God and blame Him for every evil. The Devil forces and compels, using every nasty trick in the book. He is the one who fills the heart to lie (Acts 5:3). This chief of liars, arch-conspirator, author of evil, great rebel, envenomed slanderer, apostate spirit, the most cruel of all tyrants — who attempts to blame God for all that he really is.

Successful rumours

How successful has the Devil been in his campaign of celestial rumours? The evidence is all around. Atheism and agnosticism of all kinds; God getting the blame for everything and praise for nothing; a Devil-inspired ignorance of God that denies God not only of His real nature, but also His personality, even His very existence. God is only a mockery of God: a George Burns figure croaking out his jokes; a Santa Claus image no longer believed in by adults; a pathetic persona left on the sidelines of history. Today, 'Falsehood plays a larger part in the world than truth.' (Thomas Overbury.)

An enormous tribute to the lying rumours Satan has spread about God. So successful are his misrepresentations that a belief in God is equated with irrationality. Faith is seen in opposition to common sense — something done *despite* what you know to be true. To Voltaire, observing religious faith in his time, 'Faith consists in believing not what seems true, but what seems false to our understanding.' Trust in the God of the Bible is not supposed to make any sense at all — so the Devil suggests. Such reasoning leads either to belief that makes no sense or no belief whatever — both of which achieves the Devil's aims.

And finally, 'that Wicked One' will be revealed, 'whose coming is after the working of Satan with all power and signs and *lying wonders*'. (2 Thessalonians 2:9, emphasized.) The Devil transforms himself into an angel of light, the last great trick that fools everyone who doesn't know God as He really is.

Defamed by friends

But the rumours are not believed just by those whom the Devil has blinded. Even those who claim to know God deface Him. God comes to His own — but His own receive Him not, for they too have embraced the wrong picture of God. They do not know what He is truly like. When God is asked about the wounds He has received, He answers that they are: ' " 'The wounds I was given at the house of my friends.' " ' (Zechariah 13:6, NIV.) Sadly, God's worst wounds, His most terrible defamation, come from those who think they are His friends. How? Read on . . . .

'But if you act like wild animals, hurting and harming each other, then watch out, or you will completely destroy one another.'
GALATIANS 5:15, TEV.)

'Man's inhumanity to man
Makes countless thousands mourn.'
ROBBIE BURNS.

6
INHUMAN HUMANS
Whatever happened to the Image of God?

Shamou began work in the bangle factory when she was just 5 years old. Eighteen hours a day in a dark, smoky hole, breathing in the poisons and burning her little fingers on the hot glass to save a few moments production time.

When Shamou reached 8 she was promoted to the glass-blowing section of this modern hell, still breathing in all the deathly fumes and burning her scarred hands. After working in this desperate slavery for five years she developed severe respiratory problems and had to leave. In order to survive she sold herself for a few coins to whoever would pay. Ravaged by disease and malnutrition, she ended her brief life begging on the city streets. Homeless and unwanted, Shamou had no chance. One night she lay down among all the other cast-offs of the world, and didn't wake up. Just a huddled bundle of rags, just another lifeless form to be disposed of by the collection truck, cruising the cold grey morning.

The way we are

Sadly, tragically, pitifully, this is the way humanity really is, the strangest of living beings on this planet: ready to exploit, maltreat, misuse in any and every way everything and every*one*. And why? Because we would rather listen to Lucifer than the Lord. . . .

All without a thought, without a care for the feelings and well-being of those exploited and abused, a careless disregard for others who are human beings too. The image of God is defiled, defaced and defamed in those who were made in God's image. The result: a pitiless ruthlessness that remains unmoved by others' suffering and indifferently insensitive to the most heartless cruelty. See what happens when we follow along with Operation Godsmear? No wonder so many have given up on humankind.

What is man?

'Man is a blind, witless, low-brow anthropocentric clod' (Ian McHarg), a 'degraded mass of animated dust' (Byron). Looking at the way man relates to man, some have concluded: 'Man is a brute, only more intelligent than the other brutes' (H. G. Wells), 'a mad, melancholy beast' (Nietzsche). For 'Man is to man all kinds of beasts; a fawning dog, a roaring lion, a thieving fox, a robbing wolf, a dissembling crocodile, a treacherous decoy, and a rapacious vulture' (Cowley). Hardly a pleasant zoo to spend some time in. . . .

Why is it that of all living creatures on this planet, members of that self-deluded race *homo sapiens* are the only ones to so degrade and exploit themselves? Why is it true that 'Man is the only animal to whom the torture and death of his fellow creatures is amusing in itself' (James A. Froude)? Why is it that 'The human being as a commodity is the disease of our age' (Max Lerner)?

The exploitation virtue?

Some would even take this exploitation and abuse of each other by ourselves and turn it into a virtue!

Said Nietzsche, whose philosophy was in turn exploited by the Nazis in their catalogue of horrendous exploitation: 'It is the duty of the free man to live for his own sake, and not for others. . . . Exploitation does not belong to a depraved or an imperfect and primitive state of society

... it is a consequence of the intrinsic Will to Power, which is just the Will to Live.' Jews, Christians, Gypsies — whatever — just fuel for the fires, a resource to be 'developed' and 'exploited'. Not people, human beings with infinite value, but 'raw material' to be plundered and abused. The ultimate horror: using human beings as a source of fertilizer and fat for making soap. . . .

A whole system based on exalting exploitation, following such highly 'ethical' advice as Spinoza in his work, *Ethics*: 'The primary and sole foundation of virtue or of the proper conduct of life is to seek our own profit.' Man as commodity.

Pictures of exploitative abuse

Ever the same. A few images from past and present:

Image one. A small 7-year-old boy trudges past, grimy-faced and sad-eyed, on his way through the early morning darkness to another sixteen-hour day down the coal mine. In a few moments he's gone. Only his hacking cough echoes back through the heavy, oppressive night.

Just a tiny, 'insignificant' victim of the industrial revolution, condemned to a life of penal servitude yet committing no crime, sentenced to die before he ever truly lived. And before the complaints come in that today there are laws against such exploitation, just take a look around. . . .

Image two. A woman weeps on the stand somewhere in an ancient slave market. Sold in all her entirety as a thing, an object to be used and abused, to be set to work like some mechanical robot. Only another piece of merchandise to be disposed of under the auctioneer's gavel.

Just another tragic victim, a casualty of a time when life was cheap. Another poor soul sentenced to life-long bondage, freedom-stripped and humanity-degraded.

Nobody is exploited like that today, are they? Surely slavery ended ages ago. Except nobody told those driven into economic slavery, or sweat-shop labour, or forcible prostitution. The shackles are no less real for being invisible.

Image three. A tiny baby girl, doll-like, lies bruised and battered. Little body broken with pain. Another victim of appalling child abuse, a 'thing' used as a punching bag or sex 'object' by some 'mature adult'. An ever-increasing toll that is paid by the innocent and defenceless.

Just another sobbing product of a sick and evil world where you take what you want from whoever, whenever — and who cares about them anyway? Just get what you want and ignore the consequences because I'm OK. Even if the babies suffer. . . .

Darwin's doctrine of Survival of the Fittest fits modern society well. Is it perhaps both a reflection and a rationalization of such exploitative behaviour? Whatever, people are no longer persons but resource material.

Victims all. . . . Now as well as then. Despite the vain dreams of human progress, the great keynote of the twentieth century as well as any previous age is *exploitation*. 'Ah, how unjust to nature and himself/Is thoughtless, thankless, inconsistent man!' (Edward Young.)

We may not have the child exploitation of Charles Dickens's mines and factories. The workhouse may be gone. Slavery may be officially outlawed. Torture and abuse may be condemned. *But the exploitation is there just the same.*

Turning people into things

In so many ways and in so many situations human beings turn each other into objects.

In the workplace people become cogs in the giant factory machine. A man puts the same bolt into the same hole for hour after hour, day after day, on the car assembly line. A woman sits in front of the computer screen feeding in information just like any other 'input device'. A relentless depriving of individuality, a reducing of humanity into some robot that exists only to serve the greater needs of some unthinking machine.

In the economy people equal producers and consumers, things whose products and needs are there to be exploited with a view to making profit. Corruption, sexploitation, fraud: only extreme forms of using people as objects, turning them into hard cash.

For the nation people are *subjects*. The amorphous mass of 'its' that are required to support the State, the worker bees that are there to labour and give themselves to keep the busy hive going. The oppression of the State that demands unquestioned service for its own sake — whatever political view is imposed. As one wit put it: 'Capitalism is the exploitation of man by man. Communism is the reverse.'

In wartime people are 'expendable items'. Cannon fodder, mere fighting machines, whose only reason for being is to go out there and kill some other human being to the stirring tones of martial music and strident words. All for the greater good of humanity, supposedly. So the Ayatollah sent his boy-soldiers to their deaths in the war with Iraq, promising that their 'martyrdom' in the Holy War guarantees them the sensuous joys of Paradise. And just to remind those who remain behind, the fountains of Tehran spurt, shower and cascade blood-red.

And *the future?* Some *Brave New World* in which people are pre-designed into different categories, ordained to serve out their time purely as functionaries? Alphas and Betas, Gammas and Deltas, each with a preset intelligence and social pattern, conceived in a glass dish and born from a bottle? Things in the service of some greater Thing? Exploiters and exploited in a never-ending round of degradation and inhumanism. . . .

Whether the violence is hidden or explicit, the rape of the human *person* continues. A necessary rape, for in order to carry out exploitation and atrocity effectively, the mind *needs* to see other people as things.

To the mugger a person is a target, a 'walking wallet'.

To the pornographer a person is sexual money, a lust object. 'A nicely packaged piece of meat.'

To the concentration camp guard a person is unwanted vermin, less than an animal. 'Worthless lice to be exterminated.'

Name-calling

Calling each other names! The most necessary beginning to abuse. That way consciences are eased, immoral actions excused. Suppressing conscience, listening to the cloying lies of Satan.

Most people find it hard (thankfully!) to go out and kill another human being. But call that human being an *ENEMY*, then murder becomes acceptable — even heroic. You kill for your country and the greater good of humankind, even kill for God. The man, that frail being of flesh and blood in your gun-sight, is not your friend or your brother but an enemy who deserves all he's about to get.

Not just enemies in wartime, either. The same applies to anybody you don't like or who doesn't happen to fit into your social, ethnic, or national group. That person is easily disposed of as an 'it' by name-calling. Think of all the pejorative names for those we wish to exploit, hurt and abuse. Racial slurs. National deprecations. Social innuendos. Weirdos and dumbos, crazies and freaks — using these (and any other of the far worse labels thrown around like confetti) means that they no longer have to be treated as people, at least not people like *us*. Having labelled people, they become objects, and objects don't have feelings and don't really *matter*.

Heretic burning and branding

Just like the old days of burning heretics at the stake. Another useful word, *heretic*, normally defined as someone who disagrees with you. . . . And how pleasantly attractive to the Devil's smear campaign: for what better defamation of God than for God's children to burn one another in His name!

Once the victim is declared to be a heretic, then he or she is no longer a person. And of course, there's only one thing to do with heretics — *BURN THEM IN SLOW TORTURING AGONY!* You don't need to worry about them, for if they are heretics then they have no more value than flies to be swatted. And you care about their pain as much as you do that of a swatted fly.

Branding people heretics, 'branding' being understood as 'burning and naming together'. Take the heavy iron brand. Place it in a furnace until it is red hot. Then stamp that brand into soft human flesh, and as the brand sears and blackens, the victim is labelled for all to see.

That's the way they used to treat heretics and criminals, so people would recognize them 'for what they were' and treat (or more correctly, mistreat) them accordingly. The Greeks branded their slaves with a delta mark, 'd' for 'doulos' (slave). The Romans used the same technique, using the letter 'F' for 'fur' (thief). At one time in France prostitutes were branded on the left shoulder with the fleur-de-lis symbol. In England the 1574 Statute of Vagabonds required gypsies and tramps to be branded with the letter 'V' on their breasts, a punitive law that was not repealed until 1832.

V for vagrant, T for thief, H for heretic — imposing judgement by means of a blazing brand; defining, identifying, owning, all by hurting and scarring those branded.

Today things are more subtle. Hot irons are no longer used. But the labels remain to depersonalize and misuse people exactly as society pleases. And how pleased the great campaigner is to see his diabolical Operation Godsmear have such overwhelming success in degrading and distorting the image of God in the minds of his perverted children.

Throw-away people

People are just used up. Human beings are expendable. In today's throw-away society of consumerism, people are consumed. Eaten up, sucked dry, and when eventually of no further use, junked.

Junked if you don't make the grade. Junked if your colour doesn't fit. Junked if you're too old or too young, too stupid or too smart, or if there's just too many of you. . . . Out you go: you just have to be thrown away and dumped on the rubbish heap of a polluted world.

This mentality of degradation and depersonalization fills the modern mind. Whatever doesn't suit, junk it. If the marriage doesn't work, scrap it. If the family doesn't fit, abuse them and leave them. If your friend fails to do what *you* want, break up the friendship and put it in the trashbag of wasted experiences.

Selfish

The selfish mind that makes itself in its own image, concerns itself with its own welfare, and cares not for any other person. 'The least pain in our little finger gives us more concern and uneasiness than the destruction of millions of our fellow-beings.' (William Hazlitt.)

Beings for whom only three things matter in life: me, myself and I; a selfish world inhabited by just one man.

Things before people

For people are only things. And often things mean more than people. Rob someone for money — for their money means more to you than they do. Steal your mum's wedding ring to get your daily fix, for that means more to you than the symbol of your parent's commitment. Lie about your workmate if it helps you advance your own promotion. If you can benefit from it, kill someone (and killing someone can mean far more than murder). Money, power, status, sex, possessions — whatever *thing* you consider of more value than the person you degrade, demean, exploit.

For what you can *have* means more than what other people *are*. The essence of exploitation. Exploitation that breeds merciless cruelty, heartless violence, loveless atrocity. For there is no God, at least not a God who loves and cares, and in the absence of God evil knows no limits.

Demented violence

Take a picture among all the horror of this world. From all the images of war and violence, torture and killing, take this disturbing image of pointless, demented violence. One that could even be called 'minor' in the league table of evil, but the more vivid for being seen 'live' on TV.

Take the thuggery of the British soccer supporters at the Heysel Stadium, Brussels. The mind of the mob took over, and with cries of 'Kill the Wops' and 'Smash the Dagos' the attackers hit and slashed the *Enemy*. Charging across, the insane crowd blitzed those other human beings who were no longer human beings in their minds, and ruled by rage, dehumanized themselves, until the enemy was defeated.

From the rubble the rescue teams pulled out dead and wounded *people*. Broken individual people who had real, personal names, who had wives and children, dreams and feelings, characters and personalities. Real people who wept and bled and shouted for the pointlessness of it all, the senseless carnage.

Just one example of the end result of Operation Godsmear: the degradation of God in humanity that makes humanity worse than beasts. Just one. And add to the list whatever you want. The total detachment of killing in My Lai. The child prostitutes of Thailand. Or the economic slavery of most of the Third World. The oppression of one regime after another. The denial of basic human rights. And on and on and on.

Or the intensely personal and totally senseless killing of Katrina Rennie and Eileen Duffy in Craigavon, Northern Ireland on 28 March 1991. Two teenage girls, aged 16 and 19, shot in cold blood 'because of their religion'. The newspaper report states it starkly: 'The victims were picked out by a hooded gunman who walked into the mobile shop and, in front of customers, shot dead the two girls who were behind the counter.'

Just imagine the scene. A bullet through the head because these girls are 'on the other side'. Which side hardly matters, even though the distinction is supposedly religious. The report goes on: 'Eileen Duffy's mother, Olive, told how she ran to the scene of her daughter's murder. "A fellow ran in and said there was shooting in the road. She was lying there and the blood was coming out of her head. I wonder how anybody could do that?" ' *The Daily Telegraph*, 30 March 1991.

How could anybody do that?

How Lucifer must have exulted over such mindless madness! How well it suits his purposes for self-appointed representatives of two supposed Christian communities to act in such a barbarous way. For what does such an act as *this* say about God?

Hurting each other. Using each other. Exploiting each

other. The way we *are*. But not the way we *have* to be . . . and not the way *we were meant to be*.

So what? How to resolve this? How to be truly human humans? And how to halt Operation Godsmear before we too are doing the Devil's work for him . . . .

Questions that confront all of us. But before the answers, we must first understand what such a situation of abuse, oppression and exploitation does to those who cause or permit it. Exploiters exploited. . . .

'They have rewarded evil unto themselves.'
ISAIAH 3:9.

'Sordid selfishness doth contract and narrow our benevolence, and cause us, like serpents, to infold ourselves within ourselves, and to turn out our stings to all the world besides.'
SIR WALTER SCOTT.

7
DEGRADATION'S BOOMERANG
What Operation Godsmear does to YOU

Scrooge, Charles Dickens's miserly character in *A Christmas Carol*, didn't care about anyone except himself. he used and exploited them to satisfy his own selfish desires. Debasing and degrading those around him, he debased and degraded himself until he became that mad, deformed character. Through treating others as things, Scrooge himself became a thing — a miser, a greedy hoarder of money with no compassion or tenderness. No human feelings, inhuman and self-debased; a depersonalized object of derision and loathing.

So the vicious cycle turns, ever more despicable, ever more inhumane.

Self-delusion

Self-deluded, self-centred, self-degraded: the boomerang of abuse comes back with a vengeance to wound the thrower. Piling coals upon their own heads by mistreating others, all who depersonalize their fellow human beings make themselves monsters in the process. 'Selfish people are incapable of loving others, but they are not capable of loving themselves either.' (Erich Fromm.) This human delusion is often noticed and commented on: 'The worst deluded are the self-deluded.' (Bovee.) 'Mankind in the gross is a gaping monster, that loves to be deceived, and has seldom been disappointed.' (Mackenzie.) Yet how little can anyone *do* anything about their self-delusions. . . .

Self-degradation

Strange truth: that in wounding and despising those around us we hurt ourselves the most. For 'We are all serving a life-sentence in the dungeon of self' (Cyril Connolly), with the end result that 'the wicked are brought down by their own wickedness'. (Proverbs 11:5, NIV.) The reality is: *what you do to others you do to yourself.* In every act of abuse you abuse yourself; every degradation of another contributes to your own dehumanization in a downward spiral of evil and malignancy. As Whittaker Chambers put it: 'Every man is crucified upon the cross of himself.'

Just like Newton's laws of motion in physics: every force has an equal and opposite force. In this case the force of abuse used against others rebounds upon abuser with equal destructiveness. This 'Law of Interpersonal Relationships' holds true — for human beings cannot retain their humanity if they degrade other human beings. A kind of addition to the golden rule: whatever you do to others, you are really doing to yourself.

Cheating on yourself. 'The first and worst of all frauds is to cheat one's self. All sin is easy after that.' (Bailey.)

Just like some insane kamikaze pilot from World War II, the attacker is inflicting blows upon the 'enemy' — his own ship!

How? How does this happen? Sometimes open and vicious, like torturers in some police state, or the treatment of human beings in concentration camps. But more often this process of self-dehumanization (for want of a better word) occurs in hidden, subtle ways. Take a 'for instance' . . .

What ever happened to the Good Samaritan?

In the Queens area of New York, Kitty Genovese was stabbed to death in full view of thirty-eight onlookers who watched from the safety of their apartments. While they looked with interest at the action, nobody felt involved enough to go and help. Only one person called the police, and only then after calling a friend to ask advice. Thoughts of self-preservation, conditioning by media violence and general apathy, led them to do nothing to save the screaming woman.

In experiments since, it's clear that most are like the priest and Levite in the story of the Good Samaritan and quite willingly pass by on the other side. Don't get involved is the motto.

The inability to act reflects the damage done by self-inflicted wounds. Television, for example, provides a substitute world in which the viewer is only a passive observer. Images of dramatized violence are condoned since 'they're only actors', while horrific stories on the news are absorbed without action 'because there's nothing I can do about it'.

Soap in your eyes

In the soap operas an alternative world is played out before your eyes; often a world with very different rules and results to real life. To make 'good drama', situations are developed to extremes. The storylines are manufactured and manipulated to give the viewers what they want, rather than truth or reality. Most dangerous of all, basic assumptions are portrayed as fact: moral codes are not as important as success; money and power are the highest aspirations; self is the greatest goal.

A kind of believable lying to oneself. As Dostoyevsky noted: 'Lying to ourselves is more deeply ingrained than lying to others.'

So the image machine is preferred to real personal relationships for it provides 'human interest' without involvement. A depersonalized form of one-way communication, a means of self-entertainment without any commitment or giving of oneself. TV is never too tired to respond as requested, is always ready to be interesting and entertaining, never answers back or argues. . . . A perfect mechanical 'person'. . . . An almost unconscious and unnoticed means of depersonalizing and dehumanizing. . . .

TV addiction

As a result of this 'most common of all addictions', TV influences the willing mind to view the real world as an option rather than the only reality. Though they watched a real murder, the witnesses to Kitty Genovese's bloody butchering had at the back of their mind that they could always switch off or change the channel.

Psychiatrists commenting on this case and the influence of TV violence in general have noted the damage (often underestimated) done to the brain by such images. The scene before the observers was viewed through the frame of reference in which violence 'normally' happened in their experience: the dramatic *portrayal* on TV or in movies. The perception of the murder was conditioned by such repeated viewing so that they were unsure as to its *real* nature and the necessity of intervention.

The result: a dehumanized, uncaring response from people who had so anaesthetized their compassion, so reduced their concern that the reality of such inhuman treatment no longer made any personal impact. They had conditioned themselves to a reaction of no reaction.

Sexual degradation

Such self-depersonalization operates in many areas of life. Like TV addiction, many other forms of addiction have similar effects. Self-degradation is obvious in alcoholism, drug dependency and obesity. There are other ways human beings demean and cheapen themselves by their own actions. Through being content with satisfying the physical drives, people make themselves into machine-like entities. Looking at the outside, being content with 'image' rather than true personality, society sinks to the level of glossy advertising with no substance of truth behind it. Self-image rather than true interpersonal relationships becomes the objective, the meaning and purpose of life.

As just one last example, note the self-imposed degradation of pornography. While most criticisms focus on the exploitation of others as the main evil, pornography's most insidious and abhorrent results are in the mind of the 'consumer'.

Pornography is not, as some have called it, a 'victimless' crime. The victims are all too obvious, and the mind of the practicer a greater casualty since the wound is self-inflicted. By treating others as objects of sexual gratification, the personality of the reader/viewer is corrupted. People are no longer people to be related to; and the ability to form true relationships is scarred and deformed. The self is abased and defiled in seeking to satisfy itself!

—o—

Self-concept

So much of this self-abuse results from misconceptions about human origins and nature. Self-concept is a very real *fact* of existence. how each person answers that vital question 'Who and what am I?' will dictate self-identity, behaviour and morality.

For example:

If I'm the product of genetic manipulation by alien astronauts who visited Earth in ancient times, then I'm just a scientific experiment.

If I'm the result of the chance combination of chemical compounds in the 'primeval soup', then I'm an accident, an overgrown amoeba.

BUT if I'm a thinking, personal being created by another such Being, then I am a person with individual worth.

And so on. Perceptions of ancestry and nature colour the way humanity acts and thinks. As a man thinks in his heart, so is he! (Proverbs 23:7.)

So often humanity follows the lies of Operation Godsmear and deludes itself. For if all morality, virtue, love — all 'higher thought' that is supposed to separate man from beast — came from some evolutionary 'progression', then each should only serve himself. ('True enough!' says Lucifer.) 'Such "ancestry" depersonalizes humanity — into apes and missing links, into accidental collections of meaningless molecules. There is no sense of

Being there — just pointless, absurd existence without rhyme or reason.' As W. S. Gilbert puts it in *The Mikado:* *'I can trace my ancestry back to a protoplasmal primordial atomic globule. Consequently, my family pride is something inconceivable. I can't help it. I was born sneering.'*

I can't help it. Believing like that, none of us can help it. We are the way we are; and so we are not responsible. If we act in a certain way, that's just because of the way we 'happened', nothing more. So why be held guilty of wrongdoing, why be punished, why anything? *It's not my fault. I can't help myself.*

So mankind degrades itself. It makes itself foolish by preferring to be evolutionary beast rather than created being. As Charles Darwin so strangely concluded in his *The Origin of Species:* 'From the war of nature, from famine and death, the most exalted object which we are capable of conceiving, namely, the production of the higher animals directly follows.' From the bestial conflict of the survival of the fittest, nature red in tooth and claw, came forth man endowed with virtue and intellect, compassion and sympathy, love and morals? To say that man with all his high ideals, morals and ethics developed out of this degraded picture of violent self-centredness is about as likely as a good God being created by the Big Bang!

Perhaps such ready acceptance of the evolutionist's speculation about human ancestry only reflects man's guilt. 'It's more comfortable to feel that we're a slight improvement on a monkey thin such a fallin' off fr'm the' angels.' (Finley Peter Dunne, *On the Descent of Man*.) If this is the real reason for accepting evolutionary theory, then man has really made a monkey of himself. . . .

Since 'Man, like Deity, creates in his own image' (Elbert Hubbard), what have human beings done to themselves? What have they turned themselves into? And what terrible atrocities are carried out in the name of this self-abused identity? For 'He who despises himself esteems himself as a self-despiser.' (Susan Sontag.)

If there is no final, compelling reason for moral values, for right thinking and doing, then nothing is left except that supposed evolutionary anarchy from which we emerged. All becomes 'meaningless, a chasing after the wind.' (Ecclesiastes 1:14, NIV.) 'Many men spend their lives in gazing at their own shadows, and so dwindle away into shadows thereof.' (Hare.) Everything means nothing, total and absolute nihilism. Sartre and Camus are right after all; join in with them in the theatre of the absurd. For nothing makes any sense, nothing has any real meaning.

Nothingness: a common theme to many popular songs. The assertion that 'nothing really matters', the question 'who cares if I live or die', the conclusion that 'there's no point . . .' all illustrate the bleak despair that eats at the heart of life itself. Nothing matters at all.

If that is true, then living with eyes closed, seeking only pleasure and self-gratification as accidental blobs of protoplasm is the only way. The Devil has won the battle for the mind, and if there is a God, He is either hateful or indifferent.

But if there is real meaning and purpose to life from the Life-giver, if our humanity is important and counts for something, if the higher concepts of love and trust and right are real — then NO!

Sin: a broken relationship

In all of this the evil that man does to himself illustrates the truth of what sin truly is: a broken relationship which is degrading, and which destroys in the end. If there is no God, there is no basis for morality except as a social convention, no basis for love except as mutual exploitation, no basis for truth except as a convenient assumption. Man the victim of his own victimization.

And what is man's God, if he still believes? A depersonalized being too, for in destroying himself, man destroys his image of divinity. Like the Greek gods full of immorality and corruption. . . . Or worse, some depersonalized God. A force, perhaps ('May the force be with you!'). Some machine that set the whole thing going and, like a forgetful watchmaker, has gone off and left us to it. Or is it true that God has died, and that there is no one there anymore? The eventual result of depersonalization is such an emphasis on self that there is no room for anyone else, including God.

—o—

Inevitable consequence

Sin is not just a legal concept: law-breaking. At its heart it is the very reverse of all we seek, for selfishness in the end destroys the self.

Back there in Eden, self-delusion accepted the lies of the Serpent's Operation Godsmear, and shattered the divine-human relationship. A breakdown of trust. Man no longer believed what God said and was, and no longer had confidence in Him. The end result? Death. The inevitable consequence of living out of harmony, a process of self-destruction. Then, at a great and final Day of Reckoning, unpardoned sinners are destroyed forever with unpardoned sin. (Revelation 20:14, 15; 21:8.)

'Evil will kill the wicked.' (Psalm 34:21, TEV.) The sure and certain *consequence* of such self-centred, love-denying activity rather than the sentence of doom from a hostile God. ' "Your own evil will punish you." ' (Jeremiah 2:19, TEV.)

In exercising the gift of free choice for evil, humanity has become warped and perverted. By buying into Operation Godsmear, we have turned our backs on the only One who can help us. The Divine Doctor is distrusted, His advice is ignored, His help rejected.

In smearing God, Lucifer smears us as well, for the last thing he wants is for the image of God to be reflected in us. And how well he has done: 'The heart is deceitful above all things and beyond cure. Who can understand it?' ' "For out of the heart come evil thoughts, murder, adultery, sexual immorality, theft, false testimony, slander." ' (Jeremiah 17:9; Matthew 15:19, NIV.) By indulging self, human beings are no longer 'a little lower than the angels' but have made themselves into terribly debased beings. Viewed from outside, 'Every inclination of the thoughts of his heart was only evil all the time;' 'Everyone has turned away, they have together become corrupt; there is no one who does good, not even one.' (Genesis 6:5; Psalm 53:3, NIV.)

The result? 'Sin pays its wage — death' (Romans 6:23, TEV); spiritual and moral death now, eternal death in the future. For sin *separates:* it breaks the relationship between humanity and its loving God (Isaiah 59:2; Colossians 1:21). Sin *rejects:* it no longer wants to know this God (Psalm 14:1; Romans 1:20, 21). And ultimately sin *destroys:* it wipes out the divinity in man, and in all its selfishness kills like a deadly virus (Proverbs 8:36; Hosea 13:9). And sin is at the heart of the Devil's programme of defamation: preventing a true understanding of what sin is and does, and how God can and will cure all those who come to Him. Operation Godsmear is the barrier to knowing God as He truly is and accepting His offer of salvation.

Alienated, enemies, rebels: the results of living for self. 'Human history is the sad result of each one looking out for himself.' (Julio Cortazar.) Hostile to others and to God, human beings programme themselves to self-destruct. 'Truly, man is always at enmity with himself — a secret sly kind of hostility.' (Georges Bernanos.)

Take Narcissus

Remember him? From one of the old Greek myths. So concerned about himself that he didn't even notice another's love for him. Echo, the nymph, died from a broken heart, and lived on only as the echo to others' voices.

But Narcissus, totally self preoccupied, sat down beside a clear reflecting pool. He saw his own image as if in a mirror, and fell in love — with himself! So much so that he gazed at his own face until he pined away, overcome with love for his own beauty. And on the spot where this white-robed youth loved himself to death there grew the flower that bears his name.

Self love. Self absorbtion. Complete self interest to the exclusion of others.

And the result? Self destruction, for to love only oneself is to deny all others, and paradoxically to kill all reason for existence.

Like Lucifer, whose heart became proud because of his beauty, and who tried to set his throne above God's. Like us who follow him, proud of ourselves, in love with ourselves, and about to destroy ourselves. . . .

But God does not leave mankind to its self-determined fate. Operation Godsmear has its divine answer: not in words but in actions. 'We were God's enemies, but he made us his friends through the death of his Son.' (Romans 5:10, TEV.)

' "I was born and came into the world for this one purpose, to speak about the truth. Whoever belongs to the truth listens to me. ... Whoever has seen me has seen the Father." '
JOHN 18:37; JOHN 14:9, TEV.

'God seeks comrades and claims love, the Devil seeks slaves and claims obedience.'
RABINDRANATH TAGORE.

8
THE 'I AM' AS HE IS
God's Response to Operation Godsmear

The divine knock-down

On a dry and dusty road the sun beats down, hard and strong. A little group of travellers pass the cracked rocks and shrivelled bushes, pressing hard along the rough track. Midday heat is not the time to be travelling, but needs must.

Then blazing from the blazing sky shines a light a million times brighter than the blinding brightness of the sun. A voice speaks like thunder crashing.

Supernatural meeting; a direct confrontation of divinity with humanity. A weak, rebellious human being fighting God. Knocked to ground, blinded, confused — yet still knowing what is happening, the man speaks.

The man, Saul of Tarsus, speaks for all men. 'Who are you, Lord?'

Who are you, Lord? What kind of person? God, who are you really? And from that dramatic experience comes the answer: Jesus, the one you're persecuting. Though God does at times use such direct action, is He then to be viewed as some overwhelming, hostile person? Is He threatening and violent? *What is God really like?* Who are you, Lord?

For how often do we see only what we want to see!

Fable

One of the fables from the distant past goes something like this. Once upon a time there was a totally obsessed astronomer. He was so obsessed by his star-gazing that he spent the day sleeping so that he could enjoy the marvels revealed by his telescope at night. All he could think of was the beautiful heavens, having no time for anything on this world.

He gazed for hours at galaxies and globular clusters, at binary stars and shimmering nebulae, at wandering planets and flaming comets. All this entranced him, and his thoughts were only of the heavens continually.

One of his special obsessions was the moon. He spent hours charting its waterless seas, naming craters, speculating over what, when and how. How he was fascinated by this strange other world, and how unimportant seemed the world from which he watched.

Then one evening as he scanned his precious moon in the fading light of day, he jumped with amazement. Right there in the middle of the moon was a shining dragon!

Quivering, he refocussed his telescope. Sure enough, it was still there. A strange beast with huge eyes and shimmering wings of gossamer, and green-blue body. As he watched it moved. He could scarcely contain his excitement as he ran outside.

He knocked on doors all the way down the street. 'Come and look! Come, my friends. I've found a dragon on the moon!'

Some laughed, and shut the door. But the more inquisitive came and, sure enough, as they looked through the telescope, there was the winged dragon.

'Amazing!' said one.

'Quite incredible!' said another.

And all were agreed that this was surely the greatest astronomical discovery ever. A living being on another world. History indeed! A tremendous success!

Success, that is, until one more curious than the rest took a look at the other end of the telescope and found a fly crawling about on the lens.

And the laughter at the astronomer's foolishness was greater than the excitement of his 'discovery'.

So men delude themselves, and find dragons on other worlds, without seeing their own self-deception. The 'god' of the moon — made in the image of a common house fly. . . .

The truth about God

God is better known in the present as an exclamation of anguish than as a real, personal, divine being. In the way in which human beings exploit one another, in the degrading dehumanization of humanity's very self, in the defaming and denigrating of God — the characterization of the divine-human relationship is clear: all is hostility and hate!

But that comes only as a result of the way in which we see the situation. Is it true? Is it possible that God has been defaced, and that in defacing God we have defaced ourselves in the process?

Divorce

At the heart of the pain in marriage breakup is the realization that once love was shared. And in order to defend the ego, each then makes the other evil. Evil in intention, evil in act, evil in professing love. Deception and self-deception are so clear in these most intimate of relationships, as husband and wife try to justify their positions, rationalize the fact that the one they now wish to be rid of was the one they most wanted to be with! And so they fabricate the past, and populate it with demons of their own devisings, reinterpreting every word and touch in the most negative way. 'Love' becomes 'manipulation'; 'compliments' become 'flattery'; 'intimacy' becomes 'exploitation'; 'truth' becomes 'deception' — and 'until death do us part' becomes 'until hate parts us to death'.

Sensationalistic? Over-the-top? Extreme?

No. We've seen it too often not to know. Love perverted is the most destructive force in the universe. And through this process of deception, each one becomes deceived and self-deluded, making 'truth' to suit themselves. How often does each one speak and act in self-deception: 'It was his fault.' 'I never loved her anyway.' 'She fooled me, deceived me. . . .' 'His love talk was silver-tongued lies.' 'I should have known better, but I trusted him.' 'I didn't deserve all this.' Denial replaces commitment, blame replaces acceptance, hatred replaces love. In all of this complex web of mutual condemnation runs the thread of self-deceit, made the more insistent because neither really wants to admit that they once truly loved. Self-deception, self-justification, self-defacing.

So what of God? Isn't this what we do to Him? — a very messy and painful divorce from the One who truly loves us. And how can He respond? What choices does He have?

Demonstrating truth

How little do people really want the truth! And in such a climate of distrust and deception, how does God get the truth across? How hard it is even on the human level, let alone the divine. . . .

How do we win the love and trust of an abused child?

How do we make an enemy into a friend?

How do we bring trust between Arab and Jew, Croatian and Serbian, or even Protestant and Catholic in Ireland?

Think of the difficulties of trying to persuade those who have some terrible bias or misconception. Only by demonstration can the true be revealed — assertions prove nothing.

Countering the charges

Put yourself in God's position. You're concerned to communicate and demonstrate the truth about yourself. How do you start? How do you tackle a rebellious, hostile crowd of fist-wavers? How do you let them know that they have rejected the wrong conception of yourself? Remember too that whatever you may say or do will be twisted and misinterpreted by the rebels.

Just imagine that you yourself have been the subject of

a massive character assassination. Everybody in your street shuns you and refuses to talk to you. Your friends ostracize you. Even your family ignores you.

How do you counter the charges? How do you restore your reputation? *What do you do?*

God's universe-wide family faces break-up and confusion. Does He simply call everyone together and demand unquestioned obedience? Would that work? Would that achieve the desired result? Satan the accuser has done his work well — how such a demand would be portrayed as evidence of the tyranny of God! The crisis in the family of God must be met with tactics other than demands and impositions; not that God would use that kind of method anyway.

Claims? 'I am God; believe me — I am totally loving, good and trustworthy.' Even though 'God is not a man, that he should lie,' (Numbers 23:19), how can the veracity of God Himself be assessed?

Do such assertions work? What of the Devil's assertions? How are they to be evaluated?

God is in an impossible situation: as ruler of the universe He has ultimate authority and responsibility. He is the One who decides. But only by relinquishing some of that power of decision can He gain what He most wants: agreement and freely-given love. So God does the unthinkable — He puts Himself on trial before all His created beings. More important still; He dies for *their* sins, in *their* place, that *they* may have eternal life.

Refuting the rumours

Heaven and earth are rife with rumours about God, instigated by the accuser himself, Satan. The trouble with rumours is that you can't stop them by a flat denial. You can shout till you're blue in the face: 'It's not true! I'm not like that!' But how will anybody *know?* Only by *demonstrating* what you're really like.

Claims and assertions are all very well. But what do they *prove?* As the sayings go, 'Words are cheap'; and 'Actions speak louder than words.'

So what can God do with rumour-spreading Lucifer,

who is accusing Him of being the very opposite of the total goodness He claims to be? Wipe this liar out on the spot?

Possibly. But what would that prove? Only that God is all-powerful — which is not the matter in question. It *might* also suggest to those who watch this summary execution that God *is* as Lucifer said: arbitrary, unkind, unloving; a selfish being who wishes to keep everything for Himself and who demands unquestioning obedience on pain of death.

So God has to begin the long, slow, agonizing process of proving the falsity of the Devil's charges, and revealing Himself as He is in contrast to the lies and rumours spread about Him. And, there on Calvary, He makes of Himself an offering for man's sin that eternal life might be in the grasp of every man and woman — the Devil's defeat made definite.

God on trial

God on trial. He's the accused. The one against whom the charges are brought. And often tried and convicted before he even has a chance to speak. . . .

The amazing thing is God says:

'I accept. I'm willing to place myself on trial. To allow my created beings to make up their own minds about me — whether to believe me, or the things the Devil says about me. I, Almighty God, the Judge of all, put myself in the dock, to be judged as to my very nature. The evidence will be open to all, so that every being may be able to make an informed decision. I will even allow the Devil, my principal accuser, to say and do all that is necessary to attempt to establish his claim that I am arbitrary, unfair, hostile, vindictive, selfish — whatever.

'Why do I do this? Because I want a relationship with my created children based on loving acceptance, not fearful compulsion. I want trustworthy friends, not rebellious enemies.'

The purpose of the Bible

The Word of God. A term often used simply as a synonym

for the Bible. But the term here has a far deeper meaning. It is His testimony, God's deposition for mankind's inspection. In reading God's Word it's striking how few are God's actual words. The recorded words of God spoken directly by Himself are only a small part of His book. The majority of the Bible's words are those of others as they react and respond to the God who comes to them; God's character witnesses.

More than a book of rules; more than a code to unravel mysteries; more than a map of the route to heaven — the Bible is a record of God's relationship with His creation. In particular it details how God operates in His dealings with human beings, in all kinds of situations. That said, it's clear that these situations are less than ideal for God's purposes. So pay particular attention to the character, background and understanding of the human figures in these historical records. God is always operating *in context!*

Some have trouble with that idea. God doesn't change, they say. He is ever the same. Which is true. But to use a human image, God does change His clothes depending on whom He's dealing with. A military uniform for those who need tough talking. A shepherd's cloak for those who need to be led gently and persuasively. A wedding suit for those who want the most intimate relationship with their divine Friend.

Trouble is, it's all too easy to think, when God speaks sharply, that this is His true nature. Or if He acts with apparent harshness, that He is being hostile and vindictive. Talk to someone who knows something of the Bible but is not convinced about the intentions of the loving Father and see what you get:

Uzzah; Why *did* God have to kill him for just holding the ark from falling?

Korah, Dathan and Abiram; Why did God make the earth swallow them up?

Achan; God demands his execution by stoning — and not just Achan but his wife and children too.

Antagonistic?

What kind of God is this who seems so antagonistic? And if some should seek to make some separation between the Old and New Testaments, what about Ananias and Sapphira — struck down right there in church! Or the seven last plagues of the Book of Revelation. . . .

Taken like that the Bible *does* seem to portray a God who causes death and destruction on a massive scale. What of the 185,000 Assyrians who perished at the hands of God's destroying angel?

Or is it OK because they were Israel's enemies? Surely they were God's children too?

Or all the firstborn of Egypt killed at God's command? Were they all evil? Did the children deserve to die?

Or the millions who died in the Flood? Drowned by a God who deliberately deluged the world. Was every one who died evil? Was every one who lived good?

Read without thinking, the Bible records God as the author of evil on many occasions. Those who follow the If-the-Bible-says-so-it-must-be-true-don't-ask-questions school of thought have terrible problems with a fickle and changeable God who at one moment is busy punishing (apparently) minor infractions and then (apparently again) tolerating the most heinous abuses.

But *if* God is seen as having to deal with *people where they were* and with the understanding of Himself that they had, *if* He is having to try to convince rebellious and perverted minds who really *don't* want to know, *if* He is invariably operating under conditions of crisis and deficiency — then God may be viewed with appreciation for His tolerance and love in trying to win back to trust a race of hostile enemies — by any means He could.

God spoke directly with Adam and his descendants; but the broken relationship of sin led to murder almost immediately and then to the grossest forms of evil. God had no choice but to remove sinners along with their sin, saving only the eight who would listen enough to get on board the ark!

Then God began again, trying to get His message

across, to prove Himself honourable and trustworthy. Nobody much was listening again; they were too busy building the Tower of Babel so that they could maybe escape the next flood. . . . So God chose one faithful man, and determined to make a special people who would witness well of their God. Through Abraham 'all nations of the world' were to be blessed. But Israel's success in fulfilling their divine commission was less than spectacular.

The 'I AM' God

Then God called Moses to speak for Him. 'How shall I identify you?' asked Moses. 'Tell them *I AM* sent you,' God replied. The I AM, the one and only, the pre-existent eternal One, the self-revealed God who is the sole true God. In His dealings with polytheistic Egypt, God *demonstrated* His claims in stark contrast to the gods of the lice, flies, and frogs. The all-powerful God is also the liberator from slavery — powerful images of the true nature of divine character. Yet so often this God who cares is misunderstood.

At Mount Sinai God shook the mountain to get His children's attention, filling the air with smoke and lightning and thunder. The people were terrified, and promised to listen to Him. Their promise lasted as long as their fear, and soon they were dancing and drinking in a fertility orgy around the golden calf.

God spoke through His friend Moses, who knew God much better, telling the people not to be afraid of God, that He was not hostile. But few got the message.

Then God spoke through all the long line of prophets, who tried to call His people to a better relationship with the Lord they professed to love and worship. Time and again Israel suffered, came back to God, prospered and left Him once more. Why did God allow the hard lessons? *Because that was the only language his stiff-necked, unwilling and forgetful people understood.* Not because that was His preferred method of communication.

Elijah had asked God to prove Himself before His erring people on Mount Carmel. God answered his request by pouring down fire on Elijah's offering, and the amazed people said 'The Lord he is God! The Lord he is God!' Such fireworks convinced them for a while, though the prophet ran away.

Then God met with a frightened Elijah at the mouth of a cave. And, when God met him, He was not in the whirlwind, or in the earthquake, or in the fire. He was the still, small voice. A voice that seeks to win by persuasion, not compulsion.

The record of the Old Testament is marred by humanity's feeble response to God's offers of love and friendship. Even the pleadings of God through the prophets made no lasting impact. God was still being misunderstood.

Jesus: God-revealer

And so He came Himself. Only by coming in person could God set the record straight, reveal His true nature, and convince us of His attitude towards us. Jesus did just that — He came to show warped, perverted human beings all that God really is. He revealed God in the clearest demonstration human minds could comprehend.

Jesus the God-revealer — that is the message of the gospels: that all humanity might see God as He really is, and love Him in response. 'No-one has ever seen God, but God the only [Son], who is at the Father's side, has made him known.' (John 1:18, NIV.) In His life and words, His miracles and very personality, Jesus is God. The most difficult part of belief is that this person is fully God — which is why so many heresies centre on misunderstandings of this very belief.

But Jesus must always be seen, understood, accepted as the infinite God. This child that is born to us, this son given to us, this tiny baby helpless and vulnerable in Bethlehem's manger. Apparently so minor and inferior. But never forget His titles as Isaiah 9:6 records them: 'Wonderful, Counsellor, The mighty God, The everlasting Father, The Prince of Peace.'

God with us. Truly. The Word that was there in the beginning with God, *who was and is God*. The Word made flesh, dwelling among us. The incarnate God who came showed humanity God as He is. In the life of Jesus, in all He says and does, the saving and healing God is *demonstrated*.

The gospels are full of this; that Jesus is God, and that only by looking at Him do we truly see God. The religious leaders of His time did not recognize God in Jesus, for their conception of God was very different. So they challenged Jesus that His testimony about God was not valid (John 8:13) since He was witnessing for Himself. No, said Jesus, I testify for the Father. ' "I am one who testifies for myself; my other witness is the one who sent me — the Father. . . . If you knew me, you would know my Father also." ' (John 8:18, 19, NIV.)

Seeing the Father

Even His disciples missed the point. They had confidence in Jesus, but they still did not view Him as God. If only they could have a glimpse of the Father Himself. . . .

'Philip said, "Lord, show us the Father and that will be enough for us." Jesus answered: "Don't you know me, Philip, even after I have been among you such a long time? Anyone who has seen me has seen the Father." ' (John 14:8, 9, NIV.)

For, Jesus said, ' "When he looks at me, he sees the one who sent me." ' (John 12:45, NIV.)

But because the majority had failed to perceive the truth, had misconceived God's true character, had ended up believing a lie — then seeing, they saw not, and hearing, they heard not, neither did they understand.

So God's people killed Him — for blaspheming God. *That God should be executed for being God is surely the most horrendous irony.*

Jesus: God revealed to pathetic humanity, that they might turn to Him and live. ' "When I am lifted up from the earth, I will draw everyone to me." ' (John 12:32, TEV.) On the cross Jesus shows God in His fullness. The cross is God stripped bare, naked to the gaze that all might see Him with nothing in between; no lying misconceptions, no mistaken views, no perverted understandings. The veil in the temple was ripped from top to bottom: God is open and accessible. He is revealed for all the world to see.

And *when* we see, when we come to the foot of the cross in repentant admiration, when we accept God as He is and give ourselves to Him, then and only then can we be healed from sin and saved into God's glorious and eternal kingdom.

But some see differently . . . .

Lucifer at the cross

Lucifer stands at the foot of the cross. Not like the women. Or like the centurion. Maybe more like those he inspires to cry out, 'If you are the Son of God, come down from the cross. He saved others — but He can't save Himself!' Triumphant, he calls out in a rage of pleasure:

'See — just watch Him die. The great tyrant of the universe is brought low, condemned to die like a petty criminal in the worst of all possible ways. Now this is poetic justice, for remember how He condemned me and threw me out of my high position. A taste of His own medicine. And look . . .'

He turns to his assembled legions of fallen angels, evil smile smeared broadly across his face.

'My friends, I told you we would win. This is the final proof of my case. We have the power to win. We can defeat the arch-dictator and liberate the universe. The cause of freedom cannot fail. Our long battle to tell the truth about the divine despot has finally come to this: the vindication of our moral superiority. The success of Operation Godsmear is now completely assured. Rejoice, for the victory is ours. . . .'

But as those fallen angels watch Jesus die, maybe questions come:

If God truly is a divine dictator, why doesn't He now wipe them out for murdering His Son?

If God is as they have pictured Him, why did Jesus *allow* Himself to be put to death?

Most of all, who is this God who says, 'Father forgive

them,' and promises paradise to the thief on his cross, and who eventually dies without a word of anger or recrimination, saying 'Father, into your hands I commit my spirit'?

But perhaps, in these sin-ravaged, evil-devastated minds, there exists nothing but perverted pleasure as they watch Jesus die. Perhaps their only thought is of unexpected victory, and vain hopes for the total conquest of God's universe.

Whatever — the cross remains God's clearest revelation. And that fact even penetrates the dulled intellects of the Devil's legions at the resurrection. For then, ah yes then, the true victory is revealed, and even Lucifer sees that he has unwittingly shown who he is and who God is — to all who have eyes to see!

Seeing is believing

For on the cross Jesus shows to all the universe the truth about God — that He *is* as He says He is. That the Devil is wrong in his assertions about God. That the rebellion of sin does lead *intrinsically* to death. In Christ's life and death and resurrection God answers all the questions about Himself. He does not take time saying *what* He is like, He *shows* it. For seeing is believing — seeing God as He truly is. He is the Light.

Revelation

Christmas lights. Every year a grand celebration is held in London to mark the occasion of the switching on of the Christmas lights. The crowds gather in the darkened streets, alive with anticipation. Very much a family time, mum and dad having come 'up to town' to watch the great event with their children. Little faces look up with excitement, ready for the moment the lights come on. Some well-known personality eventually throws the switch and the multi-coloured display dazzles the eyes, as the current hurtles up Regent Street and Oxford Street and all round Piccadilly Circus. 'Oohs' and 'aahs' rise from the crowd, and several thousand hands clap. The faces of the children are alight themselves, marvelling at all the shapes and figures of the lights, new every season.

Revelation. The light shining in the darkness. The coming of Christ the Light to a sin-darkened world. In the little town of Bethlehem, in its dark streets, shines the everlasting light.

Significant how often we use the image of light for understanding. Enlightenment. Illumination. He's a bright boy. Yes, he really does shine. Absolutely brilliant.

Light is what makes seeing possible. Seeing is comprehension, perception. To gain insight is to gain understanding. Jesus as the Light of the world means even more with such connotations.

But this is more than just the meaning of words. Jesus is the light that makes possible a true seeing of God, a seeing that is through the spiritual eye that leads to spiritual understanding. And then we see ourselves as God sees us, in all our 'righteousnesses' of filthy rags, and realize that God is our only hope. That's the Gospel!

Jesus reserved His strongest condemnation for those who were spiritually blind, but who claimed to see. ' "They are blind leaders of the blind;" ' he said, ' "and when one blind man leads another, both fall into a ditch." ' (Matthew 15:14, TEV.) When the Pharisees asked Him if He meant they were blind too, Jesus replied, ' "If you were blind, then you would not be guilty; but since you claim that you can see, this means that you are still guilty." ' (John 9:41, TEV.)

Jesus is, Himself, the most complete revelation of God. Looking at Jesus we can identify, then reject false perceptions of God. Jesus came to save man from sin and make possible salvation by grace, through God's gift of faith. (Ephesians 2:8, 9.) He also came so that as many as possible might have the chance to see as clearly as they could the true personality of God.

Of this the disciples say they were witnesses. John records, 'We have seen his glory, the glory of the One and Only, who came from the Father, full of grace and truth.' (John 1:14, NIV.) Peter refers to the same 'theophany' (God-revelation) of Christ on the mountain: 'We were eye-witnesses of his majesty. For he received honour and glory from God the Father when the voice came to him from the Majestic Glory . . . when we were with him on the sacred mountain.' (2 Peter 1:16-18, NIV.) This is what we all need to see and understand — the real Jesus of the gospels. Take the time to read them, discover the God that Jesus came to reveal. The God who comes to *save you and me!*

God unveiling

Revelation. Unveiling. Appearing. The message of the Bible is a theophany — an appearing of God to man as He is. 'For the grace of God that brings salvation has appeared to all men.' (Titus 2:11, NIV.) 'But when the kindness and love of God our Saviour appeared, he saved us.' (Titus 3:4, 5, NIV.)

The final book recounts the *Revelation* of Jesus Christ. Through all His words and works God is *revealing* Himself to those who look. God as He is, the great 'I AM' who was so dramatically revealed to Pharaoh, the I AM who came to be one with us: 'I have come that they may have life, and have it to the full.' (John 10:10, NIV.)

Once that is realized life is transformed. Like so many of the great scientists who suddenly gained a revealing insight into the problem they struggled with: Fleming and penicillin; Curie and radiation; Rutherford and the split atom. Even the apocryphal apple that provided Newton with such an impact, or Archimedes' bathwater!

Eureka! Life suddenly makes sense. There is purpose and direction. There is meaning and significance. There is God, He is *known*, and consequently He is loved, worshipped and admired — because without Him we are utterly and hopelessly DEAD!

God's answers

Jesus is the living illustration of God. Now God and His true nature can be seen and understood. This is the I AM as HE IS! Most especially, answering all those lies and misconceptions by His life and death and resurrection:

Is God tyrannical and vindictive? No, for He would not have come and died to save.

Is God punitive and judgemental? No, for it was not God who killed Jesus.

Does sin lead to death? It surely does.

Is God the Executioner? No, He is not.

Can God change laws, especially those of cause and effect? No, for if there had been any other way, then Jesus would not have died.

Are God's laws arbitrary? No, they are expressions of reality and eternal truth.

Is God really loving? He could not be otherwise — see what He has done.

How can the universe be secure from evil rebellion in the future? By seeing where such actions lead — to the death of Jesus at the hands of His 'friends'.

Is the Devil right? Absolutely not — for his lies lead to the greatest crime ever, the torturing murder of the Son of God at the Devil's hands.

But Operation Godsmear isn't finished. For Lucifer can still work to misrepresent — especially through those who claim to speak for God. . . .

'Nothing is pure to those who are defiled and unbelieving, for their minds and consciences have been defiled. They claim that they know God, but their actions deny it. They are hateful and disobedient, not fit to do anything good.'
TITUS 1:15, 16, TEV.

'Men never do evil so completely and cheerfully as when they do it from a religious conviction.'
PASCAL.

9
YOU ALWAYS HURT THE ONE YOU LOVE...
How God's representatives have assisted in Operation Godsmear

What was that about true love never running smooth? Unrequited love, love deceived, love betrayed. The world is full of it. From the melancholy songs of the Portuguese *fado* to the 'he/she done me wrong' of country music, from the tragic poetry of yesterday's poets to today's stark graffiti proclaiming 'she don't love me no more,' humanity expresses the searing anguish of broken love.

Poetry seemingly would be lost without it!
'And wilt thou leave me thus
And have no more pity
Of him that loveth thee?
Alas, thy cruelty.'
(Sir Thomas Wyatt, 'And wilt thou leave me thus?')
'When my love swears she is made of truth,
I do believe her, though I know she lies.'
(Shakespeare, Sonnets, CXXXVIII.)

John Donne concluded that, 'No where/Lives a woman true and fair.' Shakespeare provides the necessary balance: 'Sigh no more, ladies, sigh no more,/Men were deceivers ever.' Sir Charles Sedley summed up love's deception that is half-desired: 'She deceiving, I believing;/What need lovers wish for more?'

Same goes for prose. Thomas Hardy tells the incredible story, based on true life, of a wife auction. The tragic tale of *The Mayor of Casterbridge* recounts the sale at a fair — to a passing sailor for five guineas. Selling your beloved, trading her in. So much for love, yet once they loved. . . .

Or Hardy's *Tess*, vision of pathos and beauty, sensitive and passionate — yet ultimately betrayed.

Or John Fowles's *The French Lieutenant's Woman* — 'loved' and abandoned, bearing the name of her foreign lover, she walks the pier in the pounding storm.

Or Iago, that quintessential character of deceit and misrepresentation in Shakespeare's *Othello*.

Or Wickham's exploitation of Lydia in Jane Austin's *Pride and Prejudice*.

Or . . . . You choose your example!

Why is it that so many love and yet deceive, promise trust and yet betray? At the altar we claim to forsake all others: fidelity throughout life until death do us part. Yet what is the reality? The bitter plague of divorce, the agony of separation, and the sour harvest of damaged families and disturbed children. All because we promise faithful love and then plunge the stiletto of lies and deceit in our beloved's heart. *'You always hurt the one you love'* — and the words of the song are far from wrong. Oscar Wilde records the same sad experience in his *Ballad of Reading Gaol:*

'Yet each man kills the thing he loves,
By each let this be heard,
Some do it with a bitter look,
Some do it with a flattering word,
The coward does it with a kiss,
The brave man with a sword!'

And what of God? A God who seeks love and offers total trust? A vulnerable, self-giving, self-sacrificing God? Yes, absolutely! But this attitude is not for some of his supposed followers who seem dedicated to hurting the One they love.

Strange how so often those who claim to be God's special people have been the very ones who have disfigured the picture of God most. How God's PR assistants so often hurt and maim and distort the truth about the One they say they love. Strange.

Israel — God's chosen people, His 'children' — tried both extremes: laxity and legalism. Both were lies about the God they were supposed to be representing.

Idolatry and prostitution

At first they fooled around with the fertility gods and goddesses of their neighbours, indulging in their obnoxious practices of cult prostitution and child sacrifice. 'They went after other gods to serve them' (Jeremiah 11:10). They 'played the harlot' (Ezekiel 16:15) with these pagan gods, accepting the ideas and practices of their devotees: 'They mingled with the nations and adopted their customs. They worshipped their idols, which became a snare to them. They sacrificed their sons and their daughters to demons. They shed innocent blood, the blood of their sons and daughters, whom they sacrificed to the idols of Canaan, and the land was desecrated by their blood. They defiled themselves by what they did; by their deeds they prostituted themselves.' (Psalm 106:35-39, NIV.)

Israel still claimed to be followers of the true God. Just an 'adaptation' of worship patterns, as they might have said.

'But their words were all lies; nothing they said was sincere. They were not loyal to him; they were not faithful to their covenant with him.' (Psalm 78:36, 37, TEV.)

What image of the true God did Israel portray? A lax, impotent god who seemingly did not care what his supposed worshippers did, just another 'Baal' among all the other pagan deities around. A god to be appeased when angry, to be flattered and cajoled into being pleasant. A god who would do as you wanted as long as you appeased him with plenty of sacrifices. *Israel made God look a fool.*

Given up

Then came the bitter harvest of their idolatry. Having given up on God, He gave them up to their own devices: ' "But my people would not listen to me; Israel would not submit to me. So I gave them over to their stubborn hearts to follow their own devices." ' (Psalm 81:11, 12, NIV.)

This 'giving up' on His people was no easy thing for God. He agonized over it, as evidenced in His words through Hosea: 'Ephraim, how can I give you up? Israel, how can I let you go?' (Hosea 11:8, Moffatt.)

But ultimately, faced with an uncaring, unloving people, God had to let them go. The end result? Exile and captivity under a harsh heathen empire. A hard lesson that they needed to learn so badly.

In bondage to legalism

Then Israel returned. This time they determined there would be no mistake. God said they had to keep themselves away from such corrupting influences, to avoid compromise and spiritual adultery. Right!

So Israel cut themselves off from the other nations. They became exclusive and, in the process, self-righteous. They were the only ones who knew the truth, and they were keeping it to themselves. To make sure no one accidentally fell foul of God's holy law, they amplified it. *Formal* religious observance became their method. They had 'Fervent lips with an evil heart.' (Proverbs 26:23, NIV). As God said to them: ' "These people come near to me with their mouth and honour me with their lips, but their hearts are far from me. Their worship of me is made up only of rules taught by men." ' (Isaiah 29:13, NIV.)

They thought that by participating in the intricate and specific services, by providing the required sacrifices and offerings, they would gain favour with God and could continue as they were in 'most favoured nation' status. But God repeatedly reminded those who claimed this special relationship to Him that outward compliance was not what He wanted (Isaiah 1:13; Psalm 51:16, 17; Hosea 6:6.)

Israel developed a mechanism of rules and regulations

which turned God into some religious fanatic, arbitrary and severe, ready to punish the slightest infringement of His rigorous demands. A terrible tyrant who could only be served by blind, unquestioning obedience. *Israel made God a despot.*

God revealed

How easy it is to misunderstand God and clothe Him with human characteristics! So God came to man to demonstrate His true nature — Jesus, the incarnate God who came to reveal the Father. Israel failed to recognize in Jesus the God they worshipped, and rejected Him. This Jesus was not the kind of God they wanted, and so they disowned Him.

The early Christians had recognized God revealed and demonstrated in this Jesus. In seeing Jesus they had seen God the Father (John 12:45; 14:7, 9). They worshipped this God in spirit and in truth. But all too soon the memory faded, the picture began to be distorted. Like some fuzzy TV image, the picture of God revealed in Jesus was corrupted over time until some very strange God-concepts developed.

An iniquitous God

How? All part of the increasing acceptance of Christianity! Peculiar paradox — that as the Church went from persecuted through tolerated to accepted, its very ideas and beliefs came under outside influence and changed for the worse. The 'mystery of iniquity' (2 Thessalonians 2:7) was already at work.

Perhaps the most insidious influence was the idea converts from the other religions had of 'god'. Imported into the Church, pagan concepts of divinity tended to remake God in man's image as a being to be placated. Even by the second century Christians were praying not that their Lord should return, but that He should delay. Instead of desiring God's presence they feared Him. Instead of loving Friend He became avenging Judge. The whole concept of God had been turned upside-down!

Superstition

As a result the way was wide open for superstitious practices to replace reasoned trust in God.

Because God was pictured as hostile, believers prayed through others. Intermediaries were asked to plead with God on their behalf. Instead of Jesus being the image of God, other more tangible 'images' were introduced. At first they were designed to be pictorial representations to help the untaught masses. But all too soon the images themselves became the objects of worship — the icons of a new form of religion that did not look to the real representation of God in the life and character of Christ, but rather trusted in superstitious magic that resided in such holy relics and images.

Salvation through the Church

In this way the Church assumes responsibility for dispensing salvation in place of God, deemed unapproachable and unfriendly. The decrees of the Church replace God's laws that reveal His real nature of loving concern. Penance is introduced as a means to achieve salvation, rather than reliance on the actions of a saving God.

Worse still, believing in a vindictive and harsh God leads such believers to act in the same way themselves. For if God is antagonistic and vengeful in order to achieve His aims, then His followers can legitimately be the same. With the establishment of the Church as a secular power comes the persecution of those who refuse to assent to the Church's teachings. The most terrible torture is carried out in God's name, for the torturers believe they are only doing what God does Himself.

Violence

So interrogation leads to Inquisition; autocracy to *auto-da-fe;* cruelty to Crusade. Violence, persecution and warfare — all done in the most worthy cause of defending the Church. All in the name of the Lord — because God is supposed to be like this too. So one group massacres the other, and then in turn receives its own violent recompense. Christian history is littered with the corpses of the innocent, executed on behalf of God by His sword-wielding, fire-lighting, rope-tying friends.

Truly, claims to be God's special people are not enough. The truth is in the actions that result from this relationship. 'They claim to know God, but by their actions they deny him.' (Titus 1:16, NIV.) Actions of hate, malice and vindictiveness are clear denials of the truth about God.

Bible a mystery

Here the Bible speaks so plainly that it 'gets in the way'. It clearly teaches compliance with God's commands: 'The man who says, "I know him," but does not do what he commands is a liar, and the truth is not in him.' (1 John 2:4, NIV.) So God's Word is suppressed, or available only to those who can read a dead language, or made outdated, or simply ignored. In this way the interpreters of belief can make sure there are no 'misunderstandings'. The result: people whose beliefs are supposedly based on the Bible and yet who know little of what it contains. Interpreted by the authorities alone, the Bible becomes a hidden book of mysteries instead of God's clearest revelation to mankind.

Eternal torment?

Creeds and catechisms of all kinds replace the Bible. Teachings that reflect mistaken ideas of the real nature and character of God. As just one example, look at the imported idea of soul immortality. This concept, traceable back to the Greek philosophers, leads to such doctrines as hell and purgatory. For if the soul cannot be destroyed, then what is the eternal future of the wicked? What do such teaching say of God? Do as you're told, or otherwise you will be tortured in the greatest agony imaginable for ever and ever. No wonder the prime concern of believers was to avoid this terrible torment. Consequently they performed all the rites and rituals prescribed by the Church.

These beliefs and practices centre on a mechanistic concept of faith which sees God as some terrible ogre who lays down the law, and who only permits escape from eternal punishment on His own (very arbitrary) terms. God becomes a kind of 'thing' that is part of the system of avoiding eternal pain, a mechanical object that can be 'fixed' by the right application of certain techniques and forms. How far the defacing of God has come!

Hurting God

So what of now? Is God still being defaced by those who claim to know Him best? Is it still true that 'we always hurt the one we love'?

In a word — Yes! For the 'unbiased observer' it must be confusing — for there is so much nonsense talked about God and done in His name that the real nature of this God is hard to determine. Each Christian, by his or her very life, says: 'God is like this.'

So when anyone who claims to be a 'friend of God' says bad things about God, then the picture of God presented to the world is defaced. For Christians are 'a spectacle unto the world, and to angels, and to men' (1 Corinthians 4:9) — in the way that their lives demonstrate their conception of God.

God's name dragged through the mud

In 1987 the long-running saga of the TV evangelists began. Oral Roberts imprisoned himself in his 'prayer tower' and then sent out a message that unless he received four and a half million dollars (over eight million were eventually donated), God 'would call him home'. What does such an 'appeal' say about God? Hardly strange that Roberts was sued on the grounds that he portrayed God as a blackmailer. The *New York Times* reported that the suit claimed Roberts 'essentially alleged that he was under blackmail' with the threat that 'if Revd Roberts failed in this endeavour the blackmailer would take his life'.

Jim Bakker of the PTL ministry was implicated by fellow TV evangelist Jimmy Swaggart in an affair with a former church secretary. Later his homosexual tendencies were rumoured, again with high media attention. Bakker in turn charged yet another TV evangelist Jerry Falwell of lies and deception in attempting to ruin his ministry by being behind a 'hostile takeover'. And then, after all the 'holier-than-thou' revelations about the sexual sins of Jim Bakker, Jimmy Swaggart was himself caught 'consorting' with a prostitute. Tragedy, not so much for the figures involved, but for what those watching thought of the God they said they lived for.

For in all the recriminations and muck-raking, the real question most were asking was: 'How can people who claim to speak for God act like that?' The vicious comments, the fight for power, the opulent life-style — how do they match Christ's Gospel? What kind of God is behind all this?

Blasphemed

Tragically some of those watching from the outside have been led to ridicule God Himself. By bringing the way of truth into disrepute (2 Peter 2:2) 'the name of God is blasphemed among the Gentiles through you'. (Romans 2:24.)

It's not the scandals themselves that count for anything. It's what the participants have been *claiming:* that they are God's representatives.

What kind of God is apparently being portrayed here? A God who takes delight in His spokespersons taking money from those who can ill afford it, and using this money for all kinds of personal luxuries. A God who doesn't seem to be bothered by sin, saying, 'It doesn't matter whatever you do, I forgive you.' A God who is party to all manner of manipulation and scheming, of power-grabbing and self-exaltation. A defaced, corrupted image of God produced in the minds of many, an image that is a mockery of the truth.

Doing God's work for Him

Those who are certain they are doing God's work for Him can be worst of all. The work of the US Religious Right has been to 'put God back into the nation'. Yet their tactics and objectives do not always speak well of a God of liberty and free choice. Often their God is one who *imposes* Himself upon His servants, and *demands* blind obedience, rather than a Father who wishes His children to respond to Him out of their free, loving choice.

The more extreme 'Reconstructionists' wish to apply their rigid understanding of 'God's law' in terms of absolute civil penalties; the death penalty not only for murder and rape, but for apostasy and Sabbath-breaking. They wish to set up a 'theocratic' State based on legal enactments, so that everyone is 'forced' to obey God or face stringent punishment.

Antagonistic views

One noted Reconstructionist is even on record as suggesting that the ideals promoted by Jesus in the Sermon on the Mount were for a 'captive' people, and that when Christians achieve a position of political dominance they do not have to turn the other cheek, but may turn on any tormentor and 'bust him in the chops'. Such aggressive and antagonistic views promoted by those who believe they are following divine commands only further degrade the image of God, remaking God in the image of some divine dictator.

While these American Christians have spoken most definitely for God as they have seen Him — either the God of easy wealth and moral laxity or the harsh God of enforced obedience to legal requirements — on the other side of the Atlantic things are very different. Ask about God in England and it would be hard to escape the impression that His spokesmen seem confused.

Repudiating belief?

The ongoing debate over one Church spokesman's apparent repudiation of the reality of both the virgin birth and the resurrection has led many church-goers to wonder what they are meant to believe about God. The 1987 report on doctrine from the Church of England is entitled *We Believe in God* as if the matter needed clarification! While it is surely incontestable that the bishops do indeed accept the idea of God, apparent vacillation on points of belief causes bewilderment. As one confused commentator has written: 'It seems that nobody knows what the Church teaches any more. If the leaders don't know, how can the followers?'

God — so what?

All of which contributes to a 'So what?' attitude to things religious. The vast majority would not even consider going to a church to find answers to their questions. It would not even occur to them to try. The Church has become the place where you are married and buried. To most, organized religion is just a side-issue of an outdated and increasingly irrelevant faith, that may have worked in grandfather's time, but not now. As Clifford Longley, Religious Correspondent for *The Times* has written: 'From the churches' point of view, the most disturbing aspect of secularism is not hostility to religion or disbelief in God, but indifference to all such questions.'

God? Irrelevant and seemingly impotent. Worshipped by indifferent believers. A strange picture of God portrayed by those who claim to be demonstrating God to the world.

Little wonder then that so many have decided the God they have been presented with is simply not worth following. Faced with a monstrous tyrant or a ridiculous wimp, a lax dreamer or a vindictive legalist, or even just some kind of mechanical 'thing', many turn away and reject such 'gods', not understanding that each one is a caricature, a perversion of the truth.

No time for God

No time for God. 'God has been replaced, as He has all over the West, with respectability and air-conditioning,' wrote LeRoi Jones.

No time for God. Jules Renard concluded: 'We must be greater than God, for we have to undo His injustices.' For if God is as these Christians describe Him, say the doubters, then I want to have nothing to do with such a tyrannical (or even sadistic) person.

No time for God. Sceptic H. L. Mencken asserts that: 'Faith may be defined briefly as an illogical belief in the occurrence of the improbable.' God is a pointless theory, a ridiculous assertion that is contrary to modern science. 'God is dead,' says Nietzsche.

Such conclusions may well be unfounded and absurd. But they reflect the portrayal of God by those who claim to know of Him. A God defaced by those who are supposed to be 'on His side'!

Just like those devout believers in God who were so convinced of their own understanding of Him that when He came, they nailed Him to a cross for speaking blasphemy! Crucified afresh, God's nature, character and reputation are hurt by the ones who claim to love Him. The ultimate irony.

'For some are already turned aside after Satan.'
1 TIMOTHY 5:15.

'Ah! *Vanitas vanitatum!* Which of us is happy in this world? Which of us has his desire? or, having it, is satisfied? Come, children, let us shut up the box and the puppets, for our play is played out.'
W. M. THACKERAY.

10
THE GREAT PUPPETEER
the Devil's line-in

I remember my first Punch and Judy show so well. I was horrified! Punch's response to everything and everyone: a heavy blow over the head. . . . Not that Judy or the dog or any of the other puppets were particularly friendly. The whole show was based on violence, manipulated by what seemed (now in retrospect) to be a warped and maladjusted puppeteer.

'Only a bit of fun, of course. Not really serious. Just something to entertain the kids.'

Devil control

But on the spiritual level this is a parable of the warped control the devil has over this planet. Lucifer, the great puppeteer, has his hands inside all of us — to some degree. Whether we're glove puppets or stringed marionettes or radio-controlled dolls, the influence is there.

An uncomfortable thought. Because we like to think of ourselves as independent beings, responsible for our own choices and under the control of no one. 'I'm in charge — at least of me!' But look again, and see *what* the enemy is doing.

'Ha! So you all think you have that "freedom of choice" you're so proud of. Well, think again. Oh, yes,

sure you do have the right to decide. But it's so easy to predict the choice you will make in any situation. You see, I've had the practice of millennia, and so when I pull the string you jump. Easy as that! In fact, I almost wish for a bit more of a challenge from most of you. Just like Pavlov's dogs who were conditioned into salivating every time a bell was rung, I can manipulate you pretty well as I please.

'Ever seen a ventriloquist at work? With his hands inside the dummy, controlling its every move? Well, dummies, take a look at your controlling ventriloquist. I keep my mouth shut, you say the words. But the words are my words, said at my command. Your actions are planned in advance by yours truly, as much mine as if I had my hand inside, pulling the strings and working the mechanism. Such free beings, exercising their liberty of choice! So very amusing!'

True? Think about it. How much of your own life is determined by habit, by circumstances, by forces other than your own will? How much do *you* really choose?

Line-in

Check out the Devil's line-in — especially how he directly or indirectly influences YOU. Using all the latest techniques, he pursues his ancient plan. See how *little* of God's true image is left in us. . . .

Take Satanism. A direct assault upon God and His character. Satan saying, 'I am really best. I am the one who deserves worship. I will fulfil your desires beyond your wildest dreams — if you will worship me.' A fairly self-evident approach in the whole programme of Operation Godsmear. But one which is increasingly gaining ground in a world that doesn't know where to turn when there seems to be no God.

Or what of the occult? Far more deceptive in its dealings and, therefore, more acceptable to those who would never dream of identifying themselves with Satan. Inner eyes and pentangles and crystals (whether balls or New Age, makes no difference) — and the short cut to the 'spiritual' seems so attractive. On into spiritualism (and to cloak it further, there's even a spiritualist church) so that in trying to contact the dead (who 'know not anything', Ecclesiastes 9:5), the Devil's line-in is as clear as a hi-tech phone. He can send all the information he wants, since those listening at the other end so desperately *want* to believe it. . . .

And then there's astrology. Such a harmless activity, just reading my horoscope for fun. But think on. What really is behind those tall dark strangers but an even darker stranger! For:

If my life is determined by the stars, I'm not responsible.

If whatever I do is pre-planned, then it's not my fault.

If my horoscope says this is going to happen, then I might as well accept it.

Fatalism and total irresponsibility reign supreme. There is no sin to repent of if the stars made me the way I am. There is no morality, no reason for good, and ultimately no God — unless God is some capricious monster who just set it up this way.

Starry-eyed

A friend of mine lives exclusively by his star chart. All decisions are taken with reference to this touchstone. Without it, he says, he'd be lost. Propitious days, times of great power when planets are in the right alignment, matching influences to birth signs. . . . All this nonsense is used to control life, to make it work the way you want it to work, following the direction of the stars!

I still find it incredible that such an eminently sensible and intelligent person can buy into such a ridiculous system. I've argued it with him so often! That astrology can't possibly work, that it is unscientific, that it supposes forces from inanimate objects (planets) can work on animate beings (us), that it makes us mere robots under the influence of some (non-existent!) 'planetary force'! Even within itself it is contradictory. Did you ever compare horoscopes in different papers? See much agreement — except the general fudging of issues that means a horoscope can apply to almost anything? There should at least be some consistency of prediction. It's not there — because these 'astrologers' can't even agree among themselves.

Then again it is totally anachronistic. It is based on an out-dated view of the planets. The ones which were visible to the ancient world: Mercury, Venus, Mars, Jupiter and Saturn. That's all the astrologers count. So what about Uranus, Neptune and Pluto? For the astrologers, they just don't exist! Some believable system that chooses to ignore three planets of the Solar system just because they weren't known to the ancient world!

Most of all, how ridiculous to believe these ideas that come from pagan thoughts about these wandering 'gods' of the skies. Might as well go back to worshipping little metal idols as accept all this. If you want to bow down and pray to sun, moon and stars, go ahead. For me, I'd rather worship the One who made the sun, moon and stars. . . .

But just see how astrology does the enemy's work in the subtlest of ways, denying individual responsibility and accepting fate as the controlling force in human life.

Not God

And then there's all the weird and wonderful, the experiences of the 'paranormal', ESP and out-of-body experiences and mystic channellers and UFOs and ley lines and all the rest of the kit and caboodle of this occult-obsessed age.

It is almost as if we want to believe in <u>anything</u> as long as it isn't God.

Or if you do want to believe in God, check out the descriptions:

God has pre-ordained you to either heaven or hell. Some choice there!

God only responds to curious incantations and quasi-magical spells. What is God, some kind of witch-doctor?

God is pleased with self-induced pain and suffering — a flagellant God.

God is just an energy source. The Universe is God. We are God. Everything is God.

God tortures you for an eternity of indescribable pain to get His own back (or to 'be just').

God is whatever you want Him to be.

And there's no point in extending the list. *You* know what people say. *You* know how He is represented. *You* know how God is oh-so-often just made in our image, and what a perverted and tarnished image that is.

And the author of Operation Godsmear simply smiles and applauds our 'best efforts'.

Media God

Especially the portrayal of God in contemporary culture. Take for example the illustrations of God in the media. George Burns as God, creaking voice and all. The God of Hollywood films — distant in heaven, or ineffective Mr. Nice Guy. Monty Python — God as a divine foot that stomps on people occasionally. Or a feeble-minded truly *Ancient of Days* who has trouble remembering which millennium it is, let alone what he's supposed to be doing. Some God figure! In the meantime the evil and malevolent forces are transformed into the much more 'pleasant' offerings of 'Ghost' and 'Gremlins' and the new film genre oddly labelled as 'supernatural comedies'!

Degrading God and elevating evil. The age-old programme of misinformation. Even from those who supposedly believe. Don't need me to spell it out for you, just take the latest pronouncement on whatever aspect of belief you like: Resurrection, Virgin Birth, Miracles, Inspiration, the 'real' Jesus. What *are* some of these folk saying?! As one passing commentator said so well, 'Not much point me believing when this lot don't!'

Of course there are Christians who do express their definite faith. But since their belief in God doesn't hit the headlines, most newspaper readers would (it seems) prefer to read about non-believing bishops and non-professing prelates!

Which in itself is a commentary on the image of God in our modern world. . . .

So we end up with Christians who don't know what they believe in. Satanists who do. Witches and wizards and all manner of dealers in the occult who innocently or otherwise aid the advance of Operation Godsmear with its weight of deception. UFOs and flying saucers to confuse and intrigue, to distract and divert. A whole army of agents and assistants in the greatest misinformation campaign the universe has ever known.

Worse than any political campaign, *this* version of cosmic mud-slinging has reached truly epic proportions. A never-ending tirade of abuse and defamation that attempts to destroy God's reputation one way or another. And it's all one way — for God just takes it, waiting patiently for those who have eyes to see, and to understand. . . .

Master puppeteer

The master puppeteer is gearing up, marshalling all his forces. He is preparing the way for the ultimate deception: a world in which God is:

    a. forgotten, ignored, and irrelevant
    b. hostile, vindictive and cruel
    c. soppy, sentimental and indulgent
    d. or just plain dead!

He doesn't mind whether you want stringed marionettes or glove puppets or hand shadows on the wall: whatever way you choose, as long as you're hearing *him* and buying into *his* thought system, then the Devil is very, very happy!

Take a single 'for instance'. My friend Mark and I had gone to a party. A perfectly innocent party. Well, innocent as parties go, that is. Then things had started to slow. So our hosts suggested a few games. Board games. Trivial stuff, if you know what I mean. . . .

Even that began to pall after a while. Knowing every trivial thing just to win a pointless game does seem pretty pointless. Then from somewhere there appeared 'something a bit more interesting'. A ouija board.

'Just a board game.' Right? Wrong!

Most at that party shrugged their shoulders. 'No harm in trying it, I suppose.'

But friend Mark and I said differently. Young maybe, but we already knew the inventor of *that* particular 'game'.

The Master of the Great Impersonation Game — just another of the Devil's line-ins. A direct connection, if you like, mainlining into the mind.

So we said no. Don't try it. This is the Devil's work. And explained.

All we got were strange looks. Weird fanatics, said their eyes. And they went ahead.

And we continued too. Trying to convince them that this really was playing with fire, and that to mess around with the forces of darkness was total foolishness.

In the end, one of the girls asked the board if there were any present that the spirits wanted to leave. *In a flash the board spelled out Mark's name and mine.* The glass fairly sped over the letters — and I for one couldn't see how any of the hands could have done it like that. Besides, the people round that board didn't know our names anyway.

OK, we said. We've told you.

Yes, they said. Now the board's told you.

We left.

The Devil's great impersonation game. 'Just a game.' And how he smiles when we take part, as he deals us the cards of his own choosing. Think about it for a moment.

Spirits that babble

From his first lie to Eve in the Garden — 'You will not surely die' — right down the ages, the Deceiver has been suggesting that we have an immortal soul that even God can't destroy. You float away on some 'astral plane'; or you are reincarnated; or you float away as some ghost or whatever. And so, says the spinner of lies, you can contact the dead. Through a medium. Through some spiritist trance. Through worshipping me: Satanism. Witchcraft, voodoo, all kind of supernatural evil, from the firewalkers of the Pacific islands to the whirling dervishes of India and their face-skewering, from the sun-god human sacrifices of the Incas to the burning 'wicker men' murders of the Celts — through all of this Satan makes humanity dance to his tune as they try to find out the answer to that age-old question: what happens when I die?

And through spiritualism he has such a golden opportunity. He knows what old Aunt Joan said. He knows where Grandfather Sid hid the money. He knows the little nicknames only a married couple used. And so he exploits his information to fool the gullible that they really *are* in contact with their loved ones. And once that belief is established, then he can use that open channel of communication to get across any message he likes. And you can be sure he won't be speaking the truth about God!

Why was it that God spoke so strongly against consulting mediums, about spirits that babble and all such incantations? Because that communication is straight from the author of Operation Godsmear. Why is the Bible so clear that 'the dead know not anything'; that the dead are asleep; that the Christian hope is the resurrection and not some ghostly existence; that the 'soul' is just the breath of life given by God? Why? Because God does not want any of us to be ignorant about those who have fallen asleep, and be deceived by the archenemy.

Souled out

For if we *are* fooled, then we are wide open to the wiles of the Devil, who wants to blind us to the truth and have us believe him, and not God. But God says, 'I am the resurrection and the life'; and that is our hope, not some disembodied, transparent 'soul' existence.

How useful this eternal soul idea is to the Accuser! Put it together with a torturing God, and you end up with an eternally-burning Hell. How Satan jeers! Take a look at God, he says. What a wonderful person! Look how He treats those who oppose Him: fried alive for all eternity. Yet take another look at the Bible, and you can see how the Devil has misused it to formulate another aspect of his smear campaign against God.

No. The dead are truly dead. They have no more part under the sun. They know nothing. As Jesus made so clear, death is a sleep until the resurrection. And the great and blessed hope is resurrection into everlasting life when Jesus returns, changed in the twinkling of an eye to spend all eternity with Him.

But just look around you and see what most people believe. Operation Godsmear has done its work all too well. How easy a time the Devil has had, fooling the foolish.

Swallowing the bait

And so the fooling continues. In all innocence (maybe), swallowing the bait. Unaware of the hook, or who's on the end of the line that is so skilfully paid out to maximum benefit. Just like some fish I watched the other day. . . .

I stopped to watch an angler playing his line in the clear waters of the River Tavy near Tavistock. The water was so clear that I could even see the line under water, and the bait at the end. As I watched, a good-sized fish approached. Then along came another. And another. And a fourth. Four fish swimming in line, *queuing up to take the bait*. They almost seemed to be fighting over it. The angler hardly minded. He just went right on hauling them out. . . .

Us as foolish fish, waiting in a row to swallow the Devil's bait? Wanting to accept his misinformation, preferring to believe a lie than to be forced to live with God's truth. (2 Thessalonians 2:11.) How strange it all is! 'We lie loudest when we lie to ourselves.' (Eric Hoffer.)

Wanting the Devil's way. Preferring to live with all the lies and deceit, loving darkness rather than light. Why? Because our deeds are truly evil. . . .

And how the instigator of Operation Godsmear basks in such appreciation, wanting all the world to worship him in his arrogant usurping of the position of God. Planning and scheming, directing and controlling: truly the prince of this world.

His Worshipful Satanic Majesty, who even wants God to worship him!

Remember the scene?

Bow down, God

Jesus is half-dead from hunger. Weak and suffering, the Devil takes Him high up a mountain. From this high place the whole world is set out before Jesus. And not just the immediate present, but all that ever was and ever will be: the world in its most attractive manifestation, all the kingdoms of the world are presented in all their glory. All this in a brief moment of time. Glittering crowns, golden cities, fertile plains, luscious orchards, magnificent gardens — all this is yours, and all the people in the kingdoms, if you will bow down and worship me. What a trade! The whole world for an insignificant ceremony! And the greatest temptation is for Jesus to follow the Devil's way of achieving Jesus' mission — which was to reclaim the world.

But how foolish is this self-proclaimed 'god'! How could he ever expect the true God of the universe to bow down to him? How utterly absurd, how ridiculously impossible.

Yet this is what Lucifer the Light-bearer wants. He still fools himself, and looks for the whole world to wonder after him. . . . And he still fools all those he can, taking as many with him as he can.

Which is why God calls out: 'Be self-controlled and alert. Your enemy the devil prowls around like a roaring lion looking for someone to devour.' (1 Peter 5:8, NIV.)

So let's take stock. If we're really aware of the Devil's line-in, how he's operating his Godsmear campaign, then what should *we* do?

Remember! Remember these essentials:

- ' "From the very beginning he (the devil) was a murderer and has never been on the side of truth, because there is no truth in him. When he tells a lie, he is only doing what is natural to him, because he is a liar and a father of all lies." ' (John 8:44, TEV.)
- He comes with power and signs and lying wonders. (2 Thessalonians 2:9.)
- He wants to deceive the whole world. (Revelation 12:9.)
- He attempts to take away God's word of truth as soon as it is planted. (Luke 8:12.)
- He is the enemy of righteousness, full of deceit and

trickery, perverting the right ways of the Lord. (Acts 13:10.)

- He enters into those who finally choose him over God. (Luke 22:3.)
- Those who do what is sinful are of the Devil, for the Devil sinned from the beginning. (1 John 3:8.)

That's the bad news. We need to keep all this in mind though, for we must know the ways of the enemy. But the good news is:

- Jesus came to heal all who were under the power of the Devil. (Acts 10:38.)
- Jesus proclaimed his mission as: ' "To open their eyes and turn them from darkness to light, and from the power of Satan unto God, so that they may receive forgiveness of sins and a place among those who are sanctified by faith in me." ' (Acts 26:18, NIV.)
- Jesus promises His protection and defence, His armour by which we are 'able to stand against the wiles of the devil'. (Ephesians 6:11.)
- We are not ignorant of his (the Devil's) devices. (2 Corinthians 2:11.)
- Though the Devil sowed his tares (lies) in the wheat (truth); they will be revealed and removed at the end of the world. (Matthew 13:13-40.)
- Ultimately the deception of the Devil is proved for what it is, and 'the devil that deceived them was cast into the lake of fire.' (Revelation 20:10.)
- Through knowing God as He truly is, all who trust fully in Him 'escape from the trap of the devil, who has taken them captive to do his will.' (2 Timothy 2:26, NIV.)

In the end, God cuts the puppets' strings, and meets us face to face. . . .

'My heart says of you, "Seek his face!" Your face, Lord, I will seek.'
PSALM 27:8, NIV.

'Face to face, the truth comes out.'
ENGLISH PROVERB.

11
THE FACE OF THE INFINITE
Seeking the personal presence of God

'Was this the face that launch'd a thousand ships?' Just a face? The face that had such dire consequences for the Greeks and the Trojans. The face that so captivated Paris that he abducted its owner, Helen, and took her captive to Troy. Her husband Agamemnon, incensed by such a crime, organized the Greek expedition against the abductor. The resultant war, with its horrific loss of life, ended in the destruction of Troy. All for a face?

Revealing faces

The face. Surely the most important part of the body for communicating and understanding — because that is what is visible, the place of *expression*. It reveals so much. In so many ways, as Sir Thomas Browne observed, the face shows our true nature: 'There are mystically in our faces certain characters which carry in them the motto of our souls, wherein he that cannot read ABC may read our natures.'

Often more is said in the face than by the words spoken. The Latin writer Juvenal saw in 'The face the unerring index of the mind,' while Petronius asserted, 'From a man's face I read his character.' No wonder conversation is so difficult if the face is hidden. Nor is it surprising that the term 'two-faced' is used for those whose opinions change depending on whom they're talking to. The expression, 'To keep two faces under one hood' has a similar meaning, referring to such a 'double-faced' attitude of evil disguised under a cloak of professed religious piety. The face must be seen, and only *one* face!

For people judge by the face. They watch facial movements to gauge the reaction, to look for the unspoken thoughts. As Shakespeare said: 'Your face is a book, where men may read strange matters.'

Which explains the many sayings that refer to the face: putting on a good face; setting one's face against; flying in the face of; making faces; facing up to; shame-faced, poker-faced, bare-faced lies. . . .

The face is capable of such a wide variety of emotion and expression. That's why when a face is damaged or marred it is so tragic and terrible. Burn victims face the additional horror of avoidance and discrimination, because their distorted faces offend others. One sufferer cried on TV: 'Why can't people accept me for myself? Why does my face have to mean so much?' A sad illustration of how we judge by the face, and how important the facial expressions are. For 'All men's faces are true, whatsoever their hands are.' (Shakespeare.)

And a tragic reason why the very word 'defaced' carries such heavy meaning. The more tragic when God's face has been defaced. For the face expresses the inner character, and the defacing of God is the defacing of His true nature. How badly the distorted image man has of the face of God needs to be restored!

Horrific faces of God

Just take a few minutes to look again at the images of gods from the past. Gaze into the faces of these deities. Try to understand what they are supposed to be like.

Faces like terrifying lions. Jackal heads. Hooked-beaked birds of prey. Dragon-headed Marduk from Babylon, Sebek the crocodile god from Egypt, hideous bloodthirsty Kali from the East. Faces of supposed gods that exude malevolent hate and violent hostility. Faces of cruelty and evil, faces that inspire fear. Faces of God?

Stories too, that curdle and chill the blood. Anath was

worshipped in Canaan, a goddess who exulted in warfare and violent death, pictured soaking her clothing in the blood and gore of fallen warriors. In Babylon and Syria the 'love' goddess Astarte's lewd and obscene worship took sexual degradation to appalling depths. From the 'civilized' Greeks come stories of their god Cronos who swallowed his children at birth until he was castrated by one who escaped — Zeus. Zeus, supposedly the highest of gods, is described as having many immoral affairs, appearing in animal form to seduce human women.

The unacceptable face of 'god'.

Gods with unseeing eyes, with unfeeling hearts, with hands that cannot bless or save. Gods that are no gods; gods clothed with all the characteristics of evil. Even those who were supposed to be benevolent are corrupted by very human vices. The face of 'god' from the museum cases is a most repellent one.

Portraying God

But *God?* The true face of God? Hardly. 'To whom, then, will you compare God? What image will you compare him to?' (Isaiah 40:18, NIV.) Can God be represented in this way? The prohibition against idol making and worship is more than rule and requirement — it reflects the fact that God cannot be 'imaged' in this way. No representation of God could ever express His true nature. 'Who shapes a god and casts an idol, which can profit him nothing?' (Isaiah 44:10, NIV.)

In the following verses in Isaiah the foolishness of making god-images in this way is pointed out in a sarcastic harangue. How people cut down a tree, use some of the wood for cooking a meal, and then some to fashion an idol to whom they pray for salvation!

'Half of the wood he burns in the fire; over it he prepares his meal, he roasts his meat and eats his fill. He also warms himself and says, "Ah! I am warm; I see the fire." From the rest he makes a god, his idol; he bows down to it and worships. He prays to it and says, "Save me; you are my god." They know nothing, they understand nothing; their eyes are plastered over so they cannot see, and their minds are closed so they cannot understand.' (Isaiah 44:16-18, NIV.)

Such depictions of the face of God — His attitude and character — are truly absurd. See how much the Devil has invested in these distorted images of God as part of his Operation Godsmear. The Bible's conclusion is that: ' "Since we are God's offspring, we should not think that the divine being is like gold or silver or stone — an image made by man's design and skill." ' 'Man-made gods of wood and stone, which cannot hear or eat or smell.' ' "Ignorant are those who carry about idols of wood, who pray to gods that cannot save." ' (Acts 17:29; Deuteronomy 4:28; Isaiah 45:20, NIV.)

Foolish wisdom

Above all, the foolishness is in thinking God to be like man or animal, that His nature and character has something in common with such beings. All the supposed 'wisdom' in thinking that God can be defined in this way by man meets solid rejection from the true God, who is only known by His self-revelation. Those who claim to know God of themselves are those who, 'Although they claimed to be wise, they became fools and exchanged the glory of the immortal God for images made to look like mortal man and birds and animals and reptiles.' (Romans 1:22, 23, NIV.) What a perversion of the true face of God!

And should some think that such misconceptions about God are only from the past, look again at the many ways God is described in the modern world — or even more seriously perhaps, *not* described. . . .

God face to face

So what of the true face of God? Deep inside there is still that strong desire to look into God's face. Like Philip who asked to see the Father (John 14:8). Like Jacob who struggled with God, and then named the place 'Face of God' for, he said, 'I have seen God face to face.' (Genesis 32:30.) Like Moses speaking to God face to face, 'as a man speaks *with his friend*.' (Exodus 33:11, NIV, emphasis ours.)

Face to face, as friends. That is the image of humanity and divinity reconciled. The reason why Jesus came: and in His face, lined and disfigured though it was at times, God is revealed. Though His visage is marred (Isaiah 52:14), though He has no beauty that we might desire Him (Isaiah 53:2), through Him the face of God is revealed in human form. Jesus comes with 'A Face like my face . . . a Man like to me' (Robert Browning); taking upon Himself humanity: 'Christ Jesus: Who being in very nature God, did not consider equality with God something to be grasped, but made himself nothing, taking the very nature of a servant, being made in human likeness. And being found in appearance as a man, he humbled himself and became obedient to death — even death on a cross!' (Philippians 2:5-8, NIV.)

To look into God's face, to see Him as He is, to know from His expression that He is love in person. Hence the blessing, ' "The Lord make his face shine upon you," ' (Numbers 6:25, NIV), and the assurance 'You Lord, are seen face to face.' (Numbers 14:14.)

No wonder the phrase 'to seek God's face' became a synonym of the religious quest. The desire to be able to gaze into the face of God, to contemplate Him in His beauty, to look at the unveiled face of the Infinite One — this is the ultimate objective. Humanity, for all its cynical scepticism, still wants to 'see a glimpse of His bright face'. (Henry Vaughan.)

Like a child needing to see a parent's face after sleep, the Psalmist rests content in the assurance that: 'And I — in righteousness I shall see your face; when I awake, I shall be satisfied with seeing your likeness.' (Psalm 17:15, NIV.) For him that is enough. . . .

So to the future. In the vision of perfection, the presence of God is supreme. The veiling of sin is torn away, the separation is ended, God and His people once more are together, face facing face. 'Now we see but a poor reflection; then we shall see face to face.' (1 Corinthians 13:12, NIV.) As the climax of human desire, as the fulfilment of the highest hope, the achievement of the greatest goal is that 'They will see his face . . . .' (Revelation 22:4,

NIV.)

The revealed face of God: the full expression of the divine character, the relationship that comes with such a face-to-face meeting, eternally.

Finding God's face

So how to find God's face? Practically, realistically? Is it down to some mystical experience, a transcendental metaphysical feeling or two? How to seek the face of God?

In trying to establish the correct 'God concept' the real problem is not the mental process. Deciding from the evidence that God exists, that He may be deduced by ontological and teleological argument, is not the most significant issue. It's certainly true that the doctrines do need to be studied, that God must be correctly understood in His actions. God does need to be known in this more factual way. But there is more. *Much* more.

In relating to the true nature of God, in seeing His true face, it is exactly the *relationship* that the term 'seeking God's face' implies that is so important. Though someone may be known to be right in the more theoretical and factual sphere does not mean that he is appreciated in the area of personal relationships.

So too with God. It may be agreed that He is the summation of truth and right. But His face may be construed as stern and harsh, set like flint against the seeker. In so many ways the perceptions of those who seek God are the real determinants of the relationship. As someone once told me, 'I know I have to love God, but I don't really *like* Him.'

The need to be able to relate to God on this interpersonal level is so important. God must be considered not just on the theoretical level but in real and personal *experience*. When the Bible speaks about 'knowing God', it is using a term that is also applied to the deepest and most intimate human experience. When a man 'knows' his wife, the Bible intimates, that is the kind of knowing that humanity needs of God.

So 'seeking God's face' means coming to God without precondition and without some preliminary self-adjustment. The face is the visible evidence of personality — which is why it is so important to envisage (a 'face' word again!) God as a personal being with a face. If God had no face humanity would not be able to relate to Him effectively (how do you have a conversation or have a meaningful relationship with God as a gas cloud, for example?). Feelings of 'fear and trembling' must not prevent this personal approach to the face of God.

The invitation is to come and look at the face of this friendly God so that we will be able to relate to Him on the right *emotional* level too. Love is not a matter of facts and theories. This is where so many Christians have problems, because their image of God is so conditioned by human thoughts and experiences. Often, though the mental (brain) picture of God may be acceptable, the emotional ('heart') image is warped and twisted.

For example, if a child has been abused by its human father, the corresponding perception of God as Father will be distorted. Even though the biblical material may indeed inform and correct the theoretical image of God as Father, that child also needs emotional healing so that the proper personal relationship may develop.

Again, the teaching of doctrine may be such that though God is presented as a God of love and of salvation, the underlying emotional need to 'perform' is stressed so that the relationship is one of bargaining with an exclusive God.

People often ask if they're 'good enough for heaven' as though God was in the business of setting exams in which 'heaven certificates' were given to those who reached the required pass level. Such questions illustrate the deeper problem that God and His laws are followed as a means to achieve the desired salvation (and to escape the alternative!) without understanding that it is an intimate *personal* experience with God that is essential.

Face to face

Which is why God wants to meet people *face to face*. Only by seeing God's face can His true nature be determined. Only by knowing God can the relationship He most desires be begun. Only then can the mechanistic forms of religion be discarded, only then can God be a real Person in the believer's life. A personal, emotional relationship. God wishes to be a friend — something that is hardly possible if salvation is a bartering of penance and good works in exchange for heaven. And this cannot be achieved without spending time 'face to face' — in praying, in studying what God is saying in the Bible, in Christian meditation on the great themes of salvation, especially the cross and its meaning.

Look again at 2 Corinthians 4 — a beautifully clear description of the Gospel. Read it slowly, absorbing every word: 'Therefore, since through God's mercy we have this ministry, we do not lose heart. Rather, we have renounced secret and shameful ways; we do not use deception, nor do we distort the word of God. On the contrary, by setting forth the truth plainly we commend ourselves to every man's conscience in the sight of God. And even if our gospel is veiled, it is veiled to those who are perishing. The god of this age has blinded the minds of unbelievers, so that they cannot see the light of the gospel of the glory of Christ, who is the image of God. For we do not preach ourselves, but Jesus Christ as Lord, and ourselves as your servants for Jesus' sake. For God, who said, "Let light shine out of darkness," has made his light shine in our hearts to give us the light of the knowledge of the glory of God in the face of Christ.' (2 Corinthians 4:1-6, NIV.)

There it is! All there! I almost want to underline every word!

Check out the points:

● Because of God, we don't lose heart.

● For us, Operation Godsmear is over. We don't follow the Devil's underhand and deceitful methods, his 'secret and shameful ways'.

● We don't use deception — that's from the deceiver! — especially when it comes to God's Word. While the Devil distorts and perverts the Word of God; we speak *the truth plainly*.

● Because of the truth we speak, we demonstrate our

truthfulness and convince the conscience of all who hear.
- The veiling of the Gospel and the blindness that so characterizes this world is caused by 'the god of this age' — the Devil. That's why the Gospel does not have greater impact, because of the deliberate policy of blinding that the Devil has carried out through Operation Godsmear.
- As a result, people simply cannot see the light of the Gospel of the glory of Christ, *who is the image of God*. God is right there before them, and they can't see Him. Tragedy!
- We don't preach ourselves. The truth is not about us, it is about God. We preach the Gospel of Jesus Christ as Lord.
- The same Creator God who made the universe, who said 'Let there be light' in a physical way, has also done the same spiritually — He has made His true light (the revelation of God through His Son) shine in our hearts. In other words, we have seen the Light!
- We have this light shining in our hearts to give us the light of the knowledge of the glory of God. How awesome this is.
- But this knowledge of the glory of God is found where? In the face of Christ. *That's* where we have to go to see God as He truly is. Only there!

How much clearer could God be? How much more definite? God as He truly is has been most supremely revealed in the face of Christ. In His smiles and His tears, in His loving eyes and expression of compassion. In His grimaces of pain, and lines of sorrow. In His soft voice and winsome speech. And most clearly in the face that looks out from the cross.

Look again, my friend, at the face of Jesus on the cross. Those eyes plead with you even through the agony of twisted lips and contorted muscles. Listen again, my friend, and hear the invitation spoken through the broken voice: Come to me, accept me as your Saviour. And understand again, my friend, that as He is lifted up from the earth, He draws all to Him.

—o—

Masks

Masks are dangerous things. Highwaymen tied scarves around their heads so they would not be recognized. Today's armed robbers do the same with stockings over the face. The need is always to hide the face. . . .

At carnival time, when mask-wearing is common, crime increases. Unaware of the identity of each other, people take advantage of the situation to benefit themselves. It's hard to identify a mugger dressed in a bird outfit, or a murderer who looks like a clown. 'There is nothing that gives more assurance than a mask.' (Colette.)

Masked people. And in some ways, we all wear masks of various kinds. People prefer it that way; and have even preferred to place a mask over the face of God. That's what the enemy has done to God through Operation Godsmear — he has masked God. For in a sense, 'a mask tells us more than a face' (Oscar Wilde), and the mask the Devil has tried to put on God tells us much about the *Devil's* nature!

If a mask has been placed on God, then it's not surprising He has been misidentified. But God wants to get rid of the mask. That is why Jesus came. To unmask God, and show Him as He is. He also unmasked the Devil, and proved the kind of person he truly is. And God also wants to unmask us, and heal us from the damage the Devil has inflicted through Operation Godsmear.

Humanity unmasked

Back to the carnival. There's a story of a famous surgeon who met a hooded lady during a carnival in Alexandria. They fell very much in love during the carnival, and he proposed marriage. But she shook her head, and ran away.

The doctor spent the year trying to find her, but without success. Then at the next carnival he found her. She would not explain her absence, or her reluctance to marry, though she maintained her love for him. Finally, in a struggle, he pulled off her hood to find a face without a nose. Some terrible disease had struck, and had disfigured her beyond description.

She wept, and explained that carnival was the only

time she felt able to escape her seclusion indoors. She felt sure he would now reject her. But the doctor, though shocked, loved her the more. He determined to repair the damage done by the disease, and recreate her face so she would never again need a mask.

After much painful surgery and convalescence, the mysterious lady and the doctor were married. United in their mutual love, masks destroyed, they exchanged their vows as they looked into each others' eyes, face to face.

A brilliant image of what God does for those who will let Him. The divine healer who can remake human faces ravaged by sin's disease and lined with pain. The only one who can take away the masks of evil distortion so that man and God see each other face to face, reunited like parted lovers.

A strange truth: only as God is repersonalized can humanity be complete and truly human. For 'we are so accustomed to disguise ourselves to others, that in the end we become disguised to ourselves.' (La Rochefoucauld.)

So how?

Rather than follow ritual exercises or mystic dreamings, the reasoned approach to seeking God's face can be summarized in more practical ways. For there to be a relationship, God must be real — mentally and emotionally. Prayer is therefore not a ceremonial and formal activity, but a time of real talking, avoiding repetitive requests. God is to be spoken to as to a friend.

Then the Bible should be *read* — in as large portions as possible — intelligently and reasonably, asking such questions as, 'What does this tell me about God? What kind of person is He? What face does He show here?' If problems come up, it is better to press on and try to relate the difficult passage to other more understandable parts. Questions of personal application are useful here: 'How does this God relate to me? What does this passage tell me about my friendship to God?'

The *intimacy* of this friendship is the important aspect. A distant God is a danger: viewed as an enforcer of laws or an interrogator, an absentee landlord or an absent-minded professor, he becomes a being to be dreaded or ignored. A close and intimate God cannot be feared or misunderstood because He is *known*, He is *friendly*, He is *loved*. God and His beneficent face can be approached only through God's own self-revelation. Creation and natural revelation are a part, but only a part. Meditation and quietness can also be a helpful part of seeking God. Worship services, singing praise, reading God's Word: all are tools to lead to God.

But in the end God is not found (as if He had got lost!). He comes and reveals Himself. Can man by searching find out God? (Job 11:7.) 'Without faith (trusting God) it is impossible to please God, because anyone who comes to him must believe that he exists and he rewards those who earnestly seek him.' (Hebrews 11:6, NIV.) Then God can unveil His face, and show His true nature. As His character is revealed, like Jesus on the mountain, then God is seen as He is, transfigured before humanity, His face shining like the sun. (Matthew 17:2.) *The face of the infinite.*

—o—

Remember Narcissus, and his self-love? Falling in love with one's own face. Humanity's greatest vice is to look to self to fulfil dreams and ideals, instead of searching for the face of God, the infinite. A terrible indictment of an existence apart from God, serving only one's own depersonalized self.

But God's assurance for those who seek His face is this: 'As we look through a glass darkly, with open face beholding we become changed. And one day, when God is completely revealed, we shall be partakers of the divine nature, knowing fully, for we shall be like him, we shall be changed, and we shall see him as he is, face to face.' (1 Corinthians 13:12; 2 Corinthians 3:18; 1 Corinthians 15:51; 2 Peter 1:4; 1 John 3:2.)

> 'Face to face! oh, blissful moment!
> Face to face — to see and know;
> Face to face with my Redeemer,
> Jesus Christ who loves me so.'
> — Mrs. F. A. Breck.

'And no marvel; for Satan himself is transformed into an angel of light.'
2 CORINTHIANS 11:14.

'And the Devil did grin, for his darling sin
Is pride that apes humility.'
S. T. COLERIDGE.

12
THE FINAL SHOWDOWN
God, the Devil, and us — at the end

So let's tell it the way it is! Really. Truthfully. Pulling no punches.

The Devil has attempted the greatest take-over bid of all. In his vast strategic campaign he has tried by every means to make God into the enemy. All the dirtiest tricks. All the lying deceptions. All the perverse manipulation of minds to make them think the way *he* does. Why?

So that he can win. Be in control. Stage his *coup* and execute God — or failing that, make God so unpopular that He might as well be dead.

And we are a major part of all of this. Buying the lies. Living in the Devil's degradation. Spitting into the face of the loving God as we drive our hard nails of demonic-inspired hate into His outstretched hands. Crucifying afresh the Son of God, and putting Him to an open shame.

Comes the end

But while God allows all this to show His true nature, to demonstrate His character to a world that has so often rejected Him — the end will come.

Not by might, nor by power, but by my Spirit, says the Lord of Hosts. The Spirit that leads us into truth, the truth about God which is the essential heart of the Gospel, the good news.

So how will it be?

But before that, a few words from the sponsor of Operation Godsmear:

'So you think you can get away with it, eh? Just zap me from the face of this ridiculous planet and then smile at all your lovey-dovey friends? Won't work, you know. Not in a zillion millennia. I shall still have the last laugh — for they will serve you from fear, and not from that over-rated emotional attachment you call love that you seem to want so much. Go ahead — pull the trigger, throw the dagger, light the fires — I'm ready for you. Whatever, you've lost the argument. I _am_ right, and the universe will know that for all eternity.

'You thought you could terrorize me, eh? Typical of you, trying to enforce your way by overwhelming power. OK, I can even admit it. I _was_ frightened by your return. But so what? As you keep on saying, it's not by might or by power. It's by the truth, and I have the moral high ground. Oh, yes, I do! And even the majority of the votes. Just look around me, God, and count. Yes, count the numbers of those who have chosen my way. So much for your 'wonderful' display of evidence. Didn't convince many, did it? Why don't you admit it then? On the basis of the votes cast, I _am_ the winner. They chose me rather than you. Can't even swallow the verdict, can you?

'And now you're going to _punish_ me, aren't you? So very pleasant, this sweet God of "love", who is quite willing to spit-roast His children. How right I am to have always exposed your hypocrisy. What dictator claims to be like you — demanding "love" under pain of death? Excruciating punishment for all who refuse to love you, Tyrant of the Universe. So you say. . . .

'Not that you can _bear_ to do it, can you? Ha! All that talk of long-suffering love, not willing that any should perish, not taking pleasure in the death of the wicked — where is all that drivel now? Weeping as you stoke up the fires, I s'pose? How very _caring_ — what pious platitudes!

'It's like I said all along, you _do_ wipe out anyone who disagrees with you. You are the divine dictator, the despot of the universe. And I will call out my defiance of *you and your tyranny as you burn me alive in the flames of the lake of fire. . . . So much for justice, and as for mercy, well. . . .*

'But you just wait. I still have a few tricks up my sleeve. And in the end, yes then, then we'll see who's really right, who really has the most support. Operation Godsmear lives, right up until my last breath. . . .

The controversy is still there, right to the end. In fact, the end highlights the arguments, for the way in which God deals with His enemies says even more than the way He deals with His friends! Which has been the theme of God's dealings all along, as revealed in His book of record. The Devil's nature is clearly spelled out — and the final results of his choice are in no doubt. But what is God's part in all of this? Take another look:

Blessed hope

The *beginning* of the end is when Christ returns. The achievement of 'the blessed hope', the arrival of the promised salvation, the consummation of the Christian's greatest desire: to be with God — forever.

And how does it happen?

Literally: ' "I will come back and take you to be with me that you also may be where I am." ' (John 14:3, NIV.)

Personally: ' "This same Jesus, who has been taken from you into heaven, will come back in the same way you have seen him go into heaven." ' (Acts 1:11, NIV.)

Visibly: ' "For as the lightning comes from the east and flashes to the west, so will be the coming of the Son of Man." ' (Matthew 24:27, NIV.)

Audibly: 'For the Lord himself will come down from heaven, with a loud command, with the voice of the archangel and with the trumpet call of God.' (1 Thessalonians 4:16, NIV.)

Dramatically: 'Look, he is coming with the clouds, and every eye shall see him.' Then 'They will see the Son of Man coming on the clouds of the sky, with power and great glory.' (Revelation 1:7; Matthew 24:30, NIV.)

— and all the rest of the clear description of the Bible that includes 318 references to this glorious event!

Response

But the significance for us here is the *response*. How do people react to this? Those who are with God, following Him, knowing Him as a true and trustworthy friend look up in delight, saying, 'This is our God; we have waited for him, and he will save us.' (Isaiah 25:9.) To them the glory of the Lord is life and healing transformation as they are changed, in the twinkling of an eye, into the people of eternity (see 1 Corinthians 15).

But for the rebels, the wicked who choose the Devil's deception, for those who turn their back on God's offer of healing salvation — the light is painful and they prefer death than to come into God's presence. They call for the rocks and mountains to fall on them — they only see wrath and judgement, to them God seems only hostile and angry. (Revelation 6:16, 17; Luke 23:30.)

Same God. Same glory. Same light. Different attitudes, different relationship, different characters. But God does *not* stand as Executioner of the wicked. And if the relationship is based on love, perfect love, then there can be no fear, for fear *does* have to do with punishment! (1 John 4:18.)

How tragic that even then, even then, the loving Creator of the universe is still feared and hated, looked upon with bitterness and dread. . . .

Just like that fear of God shown by Adam and Eve — fearing God because of their belief in the lies of the Devil. Because they had listened to him, and his misstated half-truths and complete lies, the more dangerous for being so subtly mixed: 'Did God really say, "You must not eat from any tree in the garden?" ' 'You will not surely die.' 'God knows that when you eat of it your eyes will be opened.' 'You will be like God. . . .'

Evil fruits

Evil always presents itself as beneficial. The Devil does not come with the idea of sin as bad, or wrong, or negative in any way. Rather, he presents his 'suggestions' as positive, liberating, advantageous. 'You should follow my advice. I really do know what is best for you. I have your best interests at heart. This is not for my own benefit — I'm only thinking about you and your welfare. As for what God says: are you really sure? Maybe He is telling you what to do for His *own* reasons. He wants to restrict you. He is selfish — thinking for Himself. Are you really free to do what *you* want?' And so on, with those deceptive insinuations. Just look what he said to Eve — subtle, ensnaring misrepresentations that contain just enough truth to be convincing.

But once the fruit is picked, the bite taken, the bait swallowed, then, oh, yes then, the tone changes. Threats replace enticements, sour bitterness the cloying sweetness of temptation. As one who claims to know the viciousness of God, the Devil speaks on His behalf.

'Adam and Eve — you can't go back. God hates you now. You have <u>disobeyed</u> Him. I know the consequences. He's coming to get you. Run and hide. He is furiously angry with you, and as I know Him, He will cruelly torture you for what you have done. . . . Hate Him, for He first hated you. . . .'

And so the Devil continues to spin his web of lies. The arch-deceiver from the beginning continues on with his programme of misrepresentation. Down through the avenues of time. . . .

Says Jesus of His adversary: ' "From the very beginning he was a murderer and has never been on the side of truth, because there is no truth in him. When he tells a lie, he is only doing what is natural to him, because he is a liar and the father of all lies." ' (John 8:44, TEV.)

Satan lied to himself. He deceived his own mind into thinking he could be like God.

Satan lied to the angels, insinuating that God was not the kind of person He said He was. From deep and intimate knowledge, suggested Satan, he knew the truth about God: that He was hostile and vengeful, unforgiving and severe, one who ruled with arbitrary might and with selfish motives.

Satan lied to the pair in the garden, planting the seeds of doubt about God and His trustworthiness, pretending that God was withholding something good from Adam and Eve that they could take for their advantage.

And Satan lied to all subsequent generations, corrupting and defiling the image of God, making God into the very Devil himself!

Time and time again he has sown tares among the wheat, and has come and taken away the word from the hearts of those who have heard, so that they may not believe and be saved. (Matthew 13:25; Luke 8:11.)

All part of the continuing battle for the mind (of which we are not unaware! 2 Corinthians 2:11), centring on who is the true God, and the kind of person He is. For when the Devil came to tempt Christ, his primary goal was to make Christ deny Himself — by acting selfishly, presumptuously — or (the greatest point of attack) by worshipping Satan, acknowledging Satan's claims. . . . The worshipping of the false god: ' "If you worship me, it will all be yours." ' (Luke 4:7, NIV.)

The same at the end: the Devil demanding worship for the beast, with death to all those who refuse this forced obeisance. (Revelation 13:14, 15.)

The great masquerade

Like some great carnival masque, some high-society ball, some fancy-dress party is the Devil's great masquerade, with Satan impersonating God. 'And no wonder, for Satan himself masquerades as an angel of light.' (2 Corinthians 11:14, NIV.) And he will fake everything — right down to Christ's return in glory! For, 'The Wicked One will come with the power of Satan and perform all kinds of false miracles and wonders, and use every kind of wicked deceit. . . .' (2 Thessalonians 2:9, 10, TEV.)

How on earth could it happen? Only with the willing assistance of those who want to be deceived. All good (!) dictators know this only too well. Give the people what they want, and they'll follow along.

Even down to being as foolishly trusting as to drink cyanide with Jim Jones in Guyana, believing without evidence that they would gain far more through such truly *blind faith*. Why do people follow such leaders? Because they *want* to believe. And in the end, without the sure foundation of trusting God, people will willingly believe the lie. And how the Devil will smile.

Taunts

'Just look at this God. So many people prefer me! Doesn't say much for you and your reputation, does it? And how easily they are won over to my unassailable position. How weak yours must be, to have so few. See them worshipping me, God? All the world wondering after the beast. How do you feel, huh?'

How the deceiver loves to taunt God. And as the confrontation heightens, he is defiant still, right down to the end.

Right down to the very, very end. After the thousand years are over, a millennium the other side of the second coming (Revelation 20:7), the rest of the dead come to life. The rebels rebellious still. Brought back to life in a cataclysmic finale of the cosmic controversy — the ultimate demonstration of God that nothing, no nothing, can ever win these sin-hardened rebels back to love and trust Him.

End of Operation Godsmear

The final confrontation. Satan is released from his prison of circumstance, and deceives the nations for the ultimate conflict. And once again, we're not talking tanks and torpedoes. The final battle is over the same issues as the first, the war in heaven: what *kind* of person God is, and how He rules His universe. . . .

'After the thousand years are over, Satan will be let loose from his prison, and he will go out to deceive the nations scattered over the whole world, that is, Gog and Magog. Satan will bring them all together for battle, as many as the grains of sand on the sea-shore. They spread out over the earth and surrounded the camp of God's people and the city that he loves. But fire came down from heaven and destroyed them.' (Revelation 20:7-9, TEV.)

'We can do it. Look around you, friends. See how

many we are! Millions upon millions of my followers, convinced that my way is right. . . .

'Courage. Let us go and fight like truly free beings. We know we have the power, and the moral authority to depose this dictator of the universe. March on the city, and then let us see who is right! If God is as He says He is, how can He retaliate? And if He does, then let us die fighting for the truth, for who wants to serve a God out of fear? And eternity with such a tyrant? Think about it. . . .

'LIBERATION! Let us be free. Let us be true to ourselves. And let us oppose until the end. Fight on!'

But as they demonstrate their complete and utter refusal of God and His love, then God allows them their choice: to go their own way. God gives up on them, and the wage that sin pays is theirs — death through self-destruction.

No change

And yet, at the very end, though he will not and cannot change, does Satan finally see? Does he understand that even in his end, God is true and right and loving? Does the truth that every tongue confesses apply even to Satan?

'So I lose. I lose everything. And yes, I could even say that God is right. I, even I, admit it. The battle is lost — not by might or power, but by God's spirit of truth and righteousness.'

Yet there is no remorse, no willingness to change: *'But I am what I am. What I have chosen I have chosen. No ifs or buts. And truly God is shown as He truly is. But I want no part of it. How could I? His glory and love are agony to me. I want no eternity with a loving God. For I have made myself what I am, and heaven holds no pleasure for me. Let me go my own way, knowing where this leads! Give up God, and let me go. . . .'*

In the dramatic imagery of the end we must still see God working His purpose out: to reveal His true character, whatever the Devil throws at Him. The final conflict must not become the *one* time when God acts 'out of character'. God *always* acts in character — and that character is summed up in love. So when God reveals Himself as He is at the end, then this is not vindictive torture, but simply a return to how God always has been.

So at this time of God's self-revelation in all His glory — the blazing light of pure fire — then evil cannot exist. The simple, eternal truth. And it is not God's fault! The choice lies not with God, but with those who have chosen otherwise.

And so God, in the strength of His powerful and holy love, cries. As Jesus wept over Jerusalem, so God weeps over His rebellious children. This is not soft, this is the ultimate in love: letting go.

'How can I give you up, Lucifer; how can I let you go?' And in heavenly Ramah is the sound of God weeping for His most brilliant child, because he was not.

Great deception

The truth about the God of love who has so often been misrepresented, libelled and defamed. ... For in love is the greatest capacity for misunderstanding, the hardest thing to demonstrate and prove. The most powerful potential for deception. ...

In the words of William Blake:
'There is a smile of love,
And there is a smile of deceit;
And there is a smile of smiles
In which these two smiles meet.'

In Richardson's famous novel *Clarissa*, the heroine (?) wants to believe in her supposed deliverer, Lovelace. He ardently protests his love for her, which surprises Clarissa, yet encourages her to trust him. Lovelace eventually persuades her to escape with him to London, where he sets out to conquer her in earnest. Failing, he eventually overcomes her by force. After this, her belief in him is totally destroyed, and Clarissa loses her reason. She eventually dies, while Lovelace is killed in a duel. All the million-plus words of this epic novel serve to illustrate its primary theme: the misrepresentation of love.

Such is the power of an evil-inspired deception. Such is the viciousness of misrepresentation from a bitter heart.

Such is the strength of the Devil's lies.

So much for 'love' — love that lies and cheats and deceives — the Devil's corruption of the sublimest truth. This pseudo-love that in reality is self-love, concerned only with me, me, me. 'Love' that is merely the cloak of deception, the mask of manipulation, the shroud of duplicity:

'Welcome, thou kind deceiver!
Thou best of thieves; who, with an easy key,
Dost open life, and, unperceived by us,
Even steal us from ourselves.'
(Dryden, *All for Love*.)

Stealing us from ourselves. Dehumanizing the human. Defacing the face of God: the greatest weapon in Operation Godsmear. The misrepresentation of the love of the God who is love. For ' "God is love" is not one side of the truth, but the whole truth about God — there is no other side.' (J. M. Gibbon.)

No other side! Anything that does not speak well of God is never true. For 'This is how God showed his love among us: He sent his one and only Son into the world that we might live through him.' (1 John 4:9, NIV.)

As Jesus Himself said, 'If I be lifted up . . . I will draw all to me . . . .' Only by love is love awakened. So while love has the greatest capacity for deception, it also has the greatest power to speak the truth. For through the love of God, so clearly revealed on the cross, we are won back to the truth of God, the truth about God — to God Himself. 'One loves God only through knowledge, and the degree of love corresponds to the degree of knowledge.' (Maimonides.) Love is the revelation of the truth: 'We know also that the Son of God has come and has given us understanding, so that we may know him who is *true. And we are in him who is true* — even in his Son Jesus Christ. He is the *true* God and eternal life.' (1 John 5:20, NIV, emphasis ours.)

Final showdown

The final showdown. High Noon? Only one gunman stalks the streets! 'The whole world was astonished and followed the beast. . . . He blasphemes God and slanders his name.

... He was given power to make war against the saints.' (Revelation 13:3, 6, 7, NIV.)

The final showdown. That's where we are — each of us, individually. For in every aspect the vital issues of Operation Godsmear are being played out around us and in us. Whose 'side' are we on? How do we know? How do we demonstrate the controversy?

By living and breathing! We are part of the answer to the charges the Devil has brought against God: Operation Godsmear. If we are part of his great machine of falsehood, then we contribute to the defamation of God. If we live in opposition to him and his lies, then we speak the truth about God — and experience the consequences. 'We have been made a spectacle to the whole universe, to angels as well as to men.' (1 Corinthians 4:9, NIV.)

War!

For this is no academic debate. This is war! The ultimate battle for the minds and hearts of the whole universe, beings seen and unseen, the principalities and powers, the observers of the heavenly realms. . . .

What kind of image can we use for all of this? Not a war fought with weapons of mass destruction. No blazing guns or flaming missiles. No poison gas or nuclear warheads, though there is poison and the whole issue is radioactive! Not even harps turned into bows and arrows. . . .

The warfare is in the spiritual realm. In the area that is far more real than what we call physical reality. The battle is over God.

The battle is on. And the deception is almost overpowering — so that if it were possible Satan might deceive even the very elect. Fighting and lying till the end. A war in which more is gained by tricks than direct assault. . . .

The Greeks had been there years. Fighting and dying on that plain by the Aegean sea, vainly trying to conquer the impregnable fortress of Troy. All had been tried: defeat was the only achievement. . . .

So they built a horse, a huge wooden horse, and consecrated it to the goddess Athene. And then they burned their camp and pretended to leave.

Sure that their enemies had given up the struggle, King Priam of Troy inspects the huge horse on the beach, and orders that it be brought to Athene's temple in the citadel.

With great effort the horse is dragged up on rollers. The city wall has to be widened to let it through. (What great effort we expend in fooling ourselves. . . .)

Capturing an 'abandoned' Greek, the Trojans ask why the horse had been made so big. 'To prevent you bringing it into the city,' he replies. 'For if you were to do this, you would then have the power to invade and conquer Greece!' (How well the lies are suited to our convenient vanity. . . .)

Despite the prophecies of doom, the warnings, the advice to beware of Greeks even when they come bearing gifts, the horse stands proud in the middle of the citadel.

And as the moon shines it glints on the swords of the Greek soldiers as they stealthily leave the belly of the horse, to open the city gates to their companions and the orgy of destruction begins. . . .

How pointed the story! How well it describes what we have done — buying into the Devil's cleverly-disguised stratagem to destroy us — from within. Even the 'religious' card is played — the horse is dedicated to Athene, and how wrong it would be to offend this goddess. . . . How artfully the Devil clothes his deceits with the trappings of religiosity.

Remember the surprising words we began with — of celestial rumours, angelic warfare, demonic delusions? Seemed overdramatized? Maybe not now.

For those who *know*, who have unmasked the schemes, who have seen Operation Godsmear in the piercing light of Calvary — there is no mistaking evil, however well it may be disguised: 'Let no one deceive you, my children! Whoever does what is right is righteous, just as Christ is righteous. Whoever continues to sin belongs to the Devil, because the Devil has sinned from the very beginning. *The Son of God appeared for this very reason, to destroy what the Devil had done.*' (1 John 3:7, 8, TEV, emphasis ours.)

Ultimately the showdown ends in that fiery lake of self-destruction when sin pays its wage of death. Finality arrives in victory — not by might or power (for if God forces at the end, then Satan wins!). No: the pure glory of God is revealed and those who have given up on God are themselves given up. In the blazing light of God's unveiled nature the evil are consumed. (Revelation 20:9-15.) Taking no pleasure, God weeps as His children go their own way into oblivion.

Truly there is none righteous, no not one. How smeared up we are. Our desperate need is for Christ to remake us, to heal us, to rebuild the truth from the rubble of our lives of lies. Yet for those who *have* believed and trusted, have been healed and transformed — ah, this, this is just the beginning. In the welcome light of God's presence, in the wiping away of the tears, in the embrace of the Father life truly is as it should be, forever free, forever home, forever loved.

The call to Saul on the road to Damascus is the same to us: ' "Open their eyes and turn them from darkness to light, and from the power of Satan to God. . . ." ' (Acts 26:18, NIV.) The defeating of Operation Godsmear!

Jesus open our eyes. Turn us from darkness to light and from the power of Satan's lying deception to the truth of God. Do this so that we may receive healing forgiveness of sins, and an eternal inheritance with you, our Loving Lord.

13
CONCLUSION

As I write these last words I see through the darkness the faint gleams of light streaking the sky above the hills on the distant shore.

I have travelled out here to be by myself, isolated and alone. Alone in the deserted forest, on the west side of Lake Vattern in Sweden. A swirl of breeze rustles the birch leaves, and ruffles the dark surface of the water, this northern Galilee. Dreaming, if Christ came walking now, along this shore. . . .

The dawn is brighter now. Bird-calls wake the forest. A fish splashes ripples to the shore, circles glinting in the twilight. Low over the water passes the dark shape of a Hooded Crow, croaking heavily as he lumbers past.

Waiting.

Suddenly the air, the water, the land is floodlit by a golden blaze. Everything is transfigured, transformed. And in the awe of dawn, the world seems bright and new, alive to its God.

My mind races backward. The scene is black. The enveloping veil of gloom covers all, the dark of deception, of hidden things, of evil unseen. The earth shakes, the sun is blotted out, and the dim cross is etched darker still against the shrouded sky.

Then the cry pierces the blanket of doom. The veil is torn from top to bottom. Revelation, unveiling, apocalypse. 'IT IS FINISHED' echoes like a thunderclap down the halls of eternity.

What? What is finished? The ultimate revealing of God as He is, the answering of doubts about the divine nature, the assurance of the trustworthiness of the God who heals and saves. There is no more that God can do: Lucifer's lies and deceptions stand naked and exposed in the brilliant-blinding light of God as He is.

Operation Godsmear is laid bare as utter sham, a complete perversion — that like some infesting maggot-like worm of the dark shrivels and dies in the searing light of God's truth. If I be lifted up. . . .

My mind races forward. Comes another dawn. A scintillating sunrise of ten thousand suns, reflected and refracted in million upon million rainbows dancing on the sea of glass. Stand those who have trusted, believed, committed; in fullness of joy casting down their golden crowns, and singing their heart-thanks to the God who was willing even to die to show the truth.

And for all eternity, the light of proof remains. The lie, unspoken, will not be followed, for all know where that road leads — self-destruction, brokenness and the agony of God. Truth is forever chosen simply because it is truth.

And as roll the ceaseless ages of eternity, as God reveals more and more of His limitless character, as we become partakers of the divine nature, then will the promise be made complete to those who have loved and trusted such a God:

' "No eye has seen,
no ear has heard,
no mind has conceived
what God has prepared for those who love him." '
(1 Corinthians 2:9, NIV.)

'What you have done is great and wonderful, Lord God Almighty.

Your ways are right and true, king of time.

Who will not wish to reverence you and give glory to your name, O Lord?

For only you are holy.

All people will come and worship you, for your righteous actions have been revealed.'

(Revelation 15:3-5.)

Invitation

If this book has stimulated your thinking and you want to react to the author or to know more of this gracious God, then write care of the publishers:

Autumn House, The Stanborough Press Ltd., Alma Park, Grantham, Lincs., NG31 9SL, England.